HELLO, I'M A PERSON TOO!

To
Jacqueline

HELLO,
I'M A PERSON TOO!

Maggie Durran

Celebration

First published 1984
© Celebration Services (International) Ltd.

British Library Cataloguing in Publication Data

Durran, Maggie
  Hello, I'm a Person Too!
  1. Child development—Religious aspects—
  Christianity
  I. Title
  261.5′15   B1705

  ISBN 0–906309–28–X

The poem at the beginning of Chapter 6 is taken from A THOUSAND
REASONS FOR LIVING by Dom Helder Camara published and
copyright 1981 by Darton, Longman and Todd Limited, London, and
is used by the permission of the publishers.

The excerpt from 'The Seed Song' in Chapter 1 is copyright © 1977,
Church of the Redeemer, Episcopal, 4411 Dallas, Houston, Texas 77023.
All rights reserved. Used by permission.

Set, printed and bound in Great Britain for Celebration Services (Post
Green) Ltd., 57 Dorchester Road, Lytchett Minster, Poole, Dorset
BH16 6JE, by Richard Clay (The Chaucer Press) Ltd, Bungay, Suffolk

Contents

Introduction

'It's time I wrote a book; this year I'll do it.'

A sense that now is the time grew from my realising how much of what I do with children, and how much of what I have experienced with Jacqueline have a vitality and an order to it. I have asked myself many questions about this, and others have asked me questions, too. Many people have contributed to my experience: my own family, my parents, brother and sisters, my teachers and college lecturers, my fellow members of the teaching profession. My Community experiences have provided both a contribution, clarification and development of my thinking; especially I think of Sylvia Wilkes, a long-standing friend who spent many hours with me, just reflecting on our life and our children.

My Christian life has been a gradual uncovering of God's order and *logos* (word) for his creation, including us and our children. My part is to get involved in work which supports that creative word, strengthening the presence of the kingdom of God on earth. So I sift and reflect on my experience, our experience, the experiences of many friends and many teachers, to find the heart of God, his way with children.

As you read through the chapters you may begin to wonder at the many and varied aspects of a child's growth, and how any of us can possibly keep up with them. My hope is that, in reading, you will discover not a set of rules and instructions, but an attitude, a way of seeing and loving children. And through your seeing, through your loving, you will become aware of growth needs, not so much in order to provide everything a child asks for but to realise his real needs. Thus you may provide openings, opportunities for growth.

Section One

PERSONHOOD

Chapter 1
LIFE – A GIFT FROM GOD

And all creation's straining on tiptoe
just to see the sons of God come into their own.

Romans 8:22 **(J. B. Phillips)**

I am listening to an old Beatles' album, with Paul McCartney singing the haunting refrain of 'It's a Long and Winding Road'. I feel at home; these words could be my own. Getting to know God, my Father in heaven, has indeed been a long and winding road!

I grew up thinking I was no one, except possibly a nuisance when I felt I got in the way of the others, the real people. I dreamed of a time when some real people would come and claim me, and I'd find out who I really was. As a teenager, I looked for that 'special person' who would make my dreams come true. He never came; not the magic, life-shattering, super-person I dreamed of.

No, I have had a different walk, along a winding road, a spiritual walk to discover my Father in heaven. Most of my fifteen years as a Christian have been spent in renewing and reshaping a thousand crooked and deceiving perceptions that have hidden my Father from me. In many of my steps along the way a child has been the catalyst.

Long before I began to look for God, there came the day of my daughter's birth. Outside was cold and snowy January, and she was all wrapped up in white flanelette, sleeping, with curled up fingers just showing. Tears filled my eyes; this child must never feel as unloved and isolated as I did. There must be more to life for her. She was the most wonderful person I had ever met; I cried for her, that life might not turn to ashes in her mouth.

My darkness got worse. Eventually, I found God, and through all the gloomy shadows of my life let him begin to bring life. I became aware that God had breathed life into this child of mine; like a match to a tiny candle, he had given her life. I wanted her to know the Father who had given her this best gift of all. Yet, I hardly knew him myself; I could scarcely introduce them to each other.

I gave my life to God, to rescue me, for in him was life. I knew only to follow, trusting his love which I hardly felt. And I told my growing child about him.

In due course, I qualified as a teacher and Jacqueline started school. All the time I saw children, adrift, lost and isolated. I tried to tell them of God. Many were converted, but what stability was there for them, or, for that matter, for my little five year old, who went with us to all the Festivals for Jesus? Every seed of life seemed to be snatched away by the sheer weight of isolating and divisive pressures of life.

I pleaded with God, and many times found myself reading Jesus' words in John 15, about the vine.

What these children all needed was a vine, a kind of big Christian family, in which the life of Christ would be strong and rich. Into this they could come and live, literally, not in isolation and loneliness, but surrounded by friendship and love. There would be care and concern and help in such a family.

I despaired, for I could not give this to these young people. I loved them with my whole heart, but they needed more. In a family they would experience the quality of life to such an extent that they could relax and be healed and grow. They could both be loved and love. I did not know anywhere where such a family existed, so I prayed.

COMMUNITY OF CELEBRATION

Eventually I found some people who were living that kind of family life. I recognised it the moment I met them. 'This is where I will live,' I thought, 'this is where there is life.' I had no idea how God might bring me together with these people – The Fisherfolk and Graham Pulkingham; I had to leave that with God. I said nothing and then one day, a few months after that first meeting, Graham invited me to join their Community.

I have found that the family of God's people can create the home in which our children, too, learn that God is their Father. He loves them, gives them life, cares for them. Yes, there will come a time when each of our children will decide for himself whether to live his life with Jesus. Each will decide for himself what to do with his life.

POST GREEN COMMUNITY

Some of The Fisherfolk moved to Post Green and Jacqueline and I moved with them. Another Community family, but the same way of life, the same love for one another. Once more I began to work specifically with children.

Parallel to all these events, God has guided me along a particular inner walk with him. So many times when I wanted to offer Christ's life and love to another person, like when Jacqueline was born, all I could see was my own emptiness. Faith Lees once said to me, 'God's love never seems to reach you where you *feel* it.' It does now. For God has really shown me that he loves and wants *me*, and how much he cares for me and is offering me wholeness.

As I have understood and taken hold of the truth about God's love for me, I can offer truth and love to others. As 1 John says, we love because he first loved us. For me, that love had to be more than an abstract thought; it had to be, as John says earlier in the same epistle, heard and seen and touched.

It is funny, but that is also how children know they are loved, through their whole being. Through tones of voice, attitudes, affection and warmth. These are much more than words. However true the words are, where love is concerned the words can only confirm experience; they cannot speak alone.

A SEED OF LIFE

In every child, in every person, is the life that God has given. I picture life in a person as a tiny seed. It is hidden away, not simply waiting to grow, but actually weighted down by sin, so that it cannot. It contains giftedness and creativity, ability to love and be loved, ability to be a fully mature, responsible adult. Redemption enables the person to grow towards wholeness and maturity.

Sin will always be with us till we reach that new heaven and earth which are to come. But since Jesus' death on the cross, we do not have to be controlled by sin. Jesus won victory over sin and death and gave life to us.

I have met many children who seemed to have no sense of goodness in life; there seemed only to be the negative or destructive expression in them, the effect of sin. I do not mean their own sin, but also all the sin around them, which seemed to oppress and hurt them. The influence of circumstances and attitudes around them produced in such children only hopelessness, worthlessness, powerlessness and despair.

I remember one little child in particular, who seemed to demand constant attention. Her way of doing this was always doing something nasty, mean or cruel. It would have been easy to punish her constantly; easier still to get cross with her. I found it hard even to begin to love such an unpleasant child. Yet I wanted to, so I began to ask God to help me. He showed me what he loved in this little girl. I found I began to love her, too.

This child was loved by her Father in heaven. We had to discover ways to speak and act toward her that would show her that she was loveable, through our love for her; that she was wanted, by including her fully in our lives and enjoying her company; that she had the right to be herself, by our respecting her and affirming her in every way possible.

She grew to be loveable and learned to love. Also, she now knows God loves her, and she knows when he speaks to her. She has been introduced to her Father in heaven.

A PLACE TO GROW

When sin, in the form of pressures from around or selfishness from within us, does not control our life, our children can grow as whole human beings.

We have a children's song in the Community that goes:

> One must water, one must weed,
> One must sow the precious seed.
> We'll all work in unity,
> To tend the garden of love.

The song has lots of actions, of watering cans and pulling up weeds, but despite its lightness I am always reminded of the growing life that God is bringing about.

Jesus said that he did what he saw his Father doing. I see God loving and caring for children in such a way that they can grow, and I want to work with him. We see this in our life together at Post Green, and want our life to continue to be a setting where love is offered to children.

A few years ago we had a very special visitor at Post Green, whose name was Gershom. He came from Tanzania, and had a holiday with us during a long and busy tour for the Church Missionary Society. During his stay he came to supper at the household in which Jacqueline and I lived. There were several other children, too, with parents and other adults. We enjoyed getting to know Gershom, hearing of his wife and children at home, his church and his work. As the meal finished and conversation paused, Gershom looked around at us and said, 'Be careful about your children; give them life while they are with you. It is easy to be so busy with your ministry that you lose them. Then, when they grow up and leave home, God has to start from scratch.'

We have never forgotten Gershom or his words to us. As we make decisions, as we plan and minister, we consider the children. They are in the midst of our life. Life is centred on God, and our children are included in it with us.

So they are 'watered and tended', like the seed in the song, with whatever is necessary for their growth in every way. Our unity is essential in this, unity among children and adults. The deep relationships of Jesus' love, which holds us together in our family, produce this unity. It is strong and healthy love.

CELEBRATING LIFE TOGETHER

Babies and young children laugh freely when they feel loved and enjoyed in friendship. We laugh a lot at Post Green. Alex, a good friend of mine in the Community, is a guitarist and worship leader. Once in a while she gets up in front of everyone with her guitar hung around her neck the wrong way, and goes through an intricate routine in 'attempting' to get it the right way around so she can play. We have all seen it before, but still she makes us laugh till the tears roll down our faces. Then she sings us a little home-made song about some of the funny things we have done that week.

On one evening that included several small sketches and bits of drama some of our younger children presented their own play of a 'Mister Men' story. It was delightful.

We enjoy life. Enjoyment together helps people grow, adults and children alike.

Working helps us grow, too.

I have a friend called Alexander who is eleven and enjoys helping me work in the garden. Our garden is very big, and I need his help. We have planted vegetables and flowers and raked the grass, pruned the bushes and weeded.

I went away to a conference for a few days and came back expecting the lawn to have run riot in this its busy growing season. I drove in after a long journey to see the grass immaculately cut.

'Alexander mowed,' several people told me. As far as I knew he had never before used our heavy motor mower.

'He did it bit by bit, over two days,' his father explained. 'I started it for him the first time, and after that he did it by himself.'

Today Alexander and I were in the car together taking our mower to be adjusted before tackling the lawn again.

'You know,' he said, 'no one ever knew I could use the mower, but I thought about it. And when I tried, it was really good. Do you know, there must be lots of things I can do that no one would even think of.'

I could tell he had grown bigger inside.

Worship services are very special occasions in God's family. That's when we all gather to tell God how much we love him, and listen to what he has to say to us. It is a family gathering. Each Friday afternoon Post Green Community family all gather for a worship meal, the Eucharist. In this everyone shares. All adults and all children receive the bread and the wine, and the children are included throughout the service.

Last year a family who were visiting us were guests at our worship. There were three children in the family, and they were all very touched by what they experienced. Jonathan went away and wrote some words, which he brought to one of our guitarists.

'Sandy, please write some music for these words, so we can sing them all together.'

He had written:

> Jesus, Jesus, you are with me,
> You are with me.
> Jesus, Jesus, you are with me
> All night and day.
> How you love us,
> How you watch over us.

We sing the song quite frequently. Each of us feels this way about Jesus, and a child among us put our feelings into words that we can all offer to God.

A HARD ROAD

The first time we know a person is when he is born. The first time we know of him is when the mother in whom he is conceived first realises she is pregnant, and tells us. God knows that new person long before we do.

God will and does make us aware of how precious each person is to him, from the beginning. He leads us to see that person in his way. He also leads us in helping each grow into all he means him to be.

I have experienced God's faithfulness and constant love to me and to Jacqueline. Yet still my following him over these last years has been a 'long and winding road'. Hard and unrelenting it *has* seemed. Why?

My first response that very first time I looked at Jacqueline was a wish to give her wholeness in life, for her life to be rich and full and free. I wanted to give *her* a gift. I think that God had compassion on us. My love could only be full and whole as it became a gift of Christ's love. God spoke to me, and led me to a depth of fellowship with him in his family where I could begin to give the kind of love I wanted to give.

One major barrier to that development in me, was my own fear for Jacqueline. It was hard for me to believe that a distant, all-powerful God could be trusted with one so fragile and precious as Jacqueline. He might ignore her, or forget her altogether.

To begin to see how much God loves Jacqueline has taken renewal to the very depths of my inner turmoil. When I had come to a point of believing with all of myself that God loves **me**, then I could begin to trust him with Jacqueline.

So, too, for many others. Our children are often what is most precious in life for us. When God begins to renew our lives he uncovers and heals the areas where there is division and alienation within and among us. Only when among his family, assured fully of his love, can we see and know his love for each of us, and for our children. All our deepest fears, hopes and ambitions tie us to our children, who are flesh of our flesh. Renewal of

17

ourselves and our children will always bring out our greatest anxieties; love uncovers them to heal and renew.

It has been a 'long and winding road' of experience, reflection and change. I have come to see God's continuing cycle of life. For our Community, life with our children has developed in the same way; our experience together, our hearing and reflecting on God's word, renewal, change and the growth of God's life among us have all been part of this. The chapters of this book are reflections on the way we are still walking, still learning and still growing.

Chapter 2
A GIFT FROM GOD'S PEOPLE

Today a mosquito buzzed by my ear.
He said,
'I'm glad you are here in my field.'

Today God whispered a word in my ear.
He said,
'I'm glad you are here in my world.'

Maggie Durran

Several years ago, I was walking into the office building at Post Green, and I saw Val, a friend. I waved and called 'Hello' and carried on my way. At that moment, God spoke, like a voice in my ear, so clearly that I halted in my tracks. 'You didn't greet me.' As I turned and looked back along the path, I noticed that Val was holding Jenny, her one-year-old daughter. I had walked straight past Jenny, waving and calling to her mother, but had never even acknowledged Jenny's existence. She, as so many small children do, had watched a person coming, watched her say something friendly to mother and then go on. I had ignored her. With tears in my eyes I went back. God was reminding me that a child is a person.

There are so many ways to greet and meet a baby. She can hear and understand long before speaking. There's a touch and a smile, or whatever else says, 'Hello, I'm your friend.'

Jesus said, 'Whoever receives these children in my name, receives me.' (Matthew 18:5; Mark 9:37; Luke 9:47,48; *J. B. Phillips*)

God loves Jenny – a particular, individual person, named and belonging among his people. It's one thing to understand this with our minds, and another to live it out with the whole of ourselves. All of us, adults and children, have a sense of being a person. This does not come automatically but comes from living among people who offer the necessary, life-giving love and acceptance to each other. God's people begin to see how very precious life is in each other, and in their children, and decide to help each person grow fully. The start of this process is living in the present.

TO LIVE IN THE PRESENT

It's easy to spend a lot of time living either for the past or for the future. Achievements are past, ambitions are future. We may say of a five year old, 'She's finished the yellow reading book and she's going on to the blue book. . . .' We compare one child with another to see who will achieve most in the future. But what about now, the present? After all, Jesus encouraged his people not to worry about the future (Matthew 6:25–34).

Every Sunday on my way to Sunday School I drive past the Lodge household to pick up Stephen Ball and his two sons, Christopher, eight, and Matthew, five. The Lodge is a happy, busy household, where live Rowena, Chris and Shirley, plus Stephen and Lorna with their two children. There is always something exciting happening there. For one thing, the family are renovating the house; they are rebuilding bits, plastering and carpentering, scraping and Polyfilling and painting. For another, they have several cats with regular batches of kittens. So Matthew always wants to show me something special.

Matthew knows how much I value him, not least through my having time for him to talk to me, take me by the hand and show me SOMETHING SPECIAL. I leave earlier for Sunday School than strictly necessary, so I have time for Christopher and Matthew. Having time for each other in this way helps us build each other's sense of value. For me, it has meant dealing with life in a not-so-hurried way.

I am reminded of Chris telling me a story of him and Matthew. Chris calls himself an unskilled cook. While preparing supper one day and concentrating quite hard, he happened to catch sight of Matthew poking the cat! It was a kind of prodding examination. Ignoring his saucepan for a moment, Chris watched. Matthew turned jubilantly, exclaiming,

'He's got bones!'

'Yes,' responded Chris. 'Like we have bones.'

Pause.

'Did Jesus have bones?'
'Yes, he did.'
'Has the cat got Jesus inside?'
'I don't know.'
'To help him find the way when he is lost?'
'I don't know. Do you think the cat has got Jesus inside?'
'Yes, of course he has.'
'You might be right.'
'Yes.'
'Yes.'

Matthew's reflections on a recent sermon about hearing God, his awareness of his own bones and of Jesus' friendship are a joy to be part of. Such conversations can happen when we stop and listen to each other. We can leave the supper just for that moment.

God is totally present among his people, and being like him is something we learn bit by bit. He alone helps us become whole, integrated persons. The world, because of sin, doesn't normally impart a sense of value to a person. Some individuals do; some families do; but inconsistently. Yet God created us in such a way that only when we fully live out our fellowship with him and one another will we become whole, integrated people. As he renews the life of his people, this will happen. I will feel like a person and so will you. And so will the next person I talk to and the child she's holding.

Being present to each other means being open to another person's feelings. When faced with greeting a child who is sad, I must not withdraw emotionally, but rather let her feelings reach and affect me. When someone cries, do we feel like crying too? The child who tips the pot of water over her painting is heart-broken. Someone who feels her disappointment deeply can say, 'Can I help you?' The child feels known and loved. She feels understood and received.

When not emotionally present as I walk up to a child and give her a hug, I might as well hug a lamp-post. If I'm not present to her with my feelings, to share her feelings with her and she with me, I'm behaving as if we were things, not people.

My feelings will touch and affect others, too. In talking of love, in Romans 12, Paul says, 'Be happy with those who are happy, weep with those who weep.' Jesus challenged the Pharisees who would not identify with the feelings of others (Luke 7:32).

21

Being present to receive one another also means to understand, to be conscious and present with our minds.

At the end of every school day Jacqueline catches the bus to Lytchett Minster, where our Community offices are. This is the nearest she can get to our house, which lies off a little country lane further away. So she comes into my office for us to go home together in our car. The door opens.

'Mum, guess what . . .?'

Am I going to grunt and continue my project, or will I give her all my attention for a minute before finishing my work?

What's your first response when the children rush in? I used to grunt abstractedly. Then Jacqueline would get cross and I would get cross in return. Now I am working on real listening.

Many people have jumbled thoughts, and the words come out in a way not always intended. In conversation, questions can be asked and the thoughts sorted out. Real listening and conversation help children sort out their thoughts. As they grapple with communication and thinking skills, children are not always logical. Real listening takes time and concentration. If I only wait for the child to finish 'rattling on' so I can say what I want to say, she might as well be a record; a thing, not a person.

When people are consciously and emotionally present to one another, their relationship becomes creative. The kind of creativity God gave human beings is sparked between them. And what happens between them will have repercussions elsewhere.

An example: As I walked into church, a friend, Ian, greeted me. That greeting and what he said changed what I did next, for as a result Ian helped me carry the boxes I was bringing with me and we began to set up my workshop together. When we meet one another fully, what we had expected to do might well change. Our attitudes will change, our plans will change, and our pictures of God and of life will, too.

Another example: Lydia is ten. My plan was to call at their house to see her father. I knocked at the door, and Lydia answered. I could have been so busy going to see her father that I simply said, 'Hello, Lydia, is your Dad in?' and ignored her. Or I could have said, 'Hello, Lydia, how are you? What's been happening today?' She could have had all kinds of things to tell me, that, if I really listened, would have changed the order of my day. Perhaps going to see the guinea pigs before I saw Lydia's father.

Or Lydia might have said, 'Daddy's busy at the moment.' Would I have gone away at once or would I have talked to Lydia for a while?

Sometimes, as part of my reflection on the day, before I go to bed I think back over the people I met. I often find there was someone I did not really receive and wish I had. I can repair that later:

'Debbie, I wish I could get to know you more. Would you like to come to supper one evening?'

LISTENING AND COMMUNICATING

When people in a family and in a church want to receive and be present to one another, how will it happen?

The first step is listening to everybody, the children as well as the adults, with our minds *and* feelings.

The next is speaking out for ourselves as others listen.

'How do I know what I think till I hear what I say?' I am like that and it seems that nearly everyone else feels the same. And we are all a bit afraid of being misunderstood. A slower moving discussion helps, with time for each person to say what she wants and think about what she has said. Having time to experience caring and loving reflection on life helps each person choose to tell what she is really thinking and feeling.

Let me give you an example. Our Community is governed by a Chapter. This is a group of people who meet and deliberate and plan life together. We meet in the Drawing Room of Post Green House.

Last Sunday we were trying to make some important decisions and I found myself saying:

'I hate to disagree with everyone, but I am not really sure we should do this yet.'

The discussion moved on a little, and then I realised I wanted to say something else.

'I have realised, having said I disagree, that I don't, really. I think I am going slowly because I feel sad about the family that is leaving the Community. I actually agree with the contents of the decision we are considering.' It was hard for me to say that, but the other members had time for me. The next day two people

23

came to say they had felt the same and had been glad I had said it. I felt received and known.

There are certain behavioural patterns learned from the world that can prevent adults valuing one another as persons, and prevent children from genuinely communicating with adults. Sometimes they are even corrected as they imitate the attitudes and behaviour they see.

From time to time I have found myself thinking, 'I know what I am going to do. If I say nothing and just get on with it, no one else will have a chance to change it from what I want.' That is not at all affirming to my friends, because it disregards what they might think and feel. This does happen quite frequently with children. For instance, the child ignores it when the adult calls. The adult, however, may well have set the example.

What shall I do when I am sure *I* know best? It is sometimes hard to see that truth is made up from all that each of us brings. None of us has all the knowledge or sees the whole picture; we each see part of it. Big parts or little parts, we all see some and we all bring some. When we look at a car from opposite sides of the road we see differences, but both are true pictures of the same car. When we really listen to each other, together we have a bigger picture of truth. However much any one person knows, the picture will always be bigger after listening to others.

So how can we in our decision-making take everyone into account? Only by listening to them. Do we really listen to the people who are different from us? Or do we not, in fact, often ignore and avoid them? Let me give an example: Whose group do I choose to be in, or whose partner do I choose to be? Is she my kind of person?

Recently I went to a Serendipity Training Day run by Scripture Union. Lyman Coleman said something like this:

'I want you to find a partner. Look for someone whom you don't know. Someone you have never met, who dresses all wrong and looks as if she likes all the things you don't. The person you would never pick.'

My partner, it turned out, listened to Radio 2 and Radio 4. I listen to Radio 1. She wore a summer skirt, and was altogether smartly dressed. I was wearing jeans and boots and was very casual. But we had a very good time together.

Persistence in overcoming these barriers will create an atmosphere where personhood will be experienced by all concerned. Persistence and determination will get beyond the place where a person feels pushed around by society, like traffic by the traffic lights. There is listening, empathy and opportunity for various viewpoints to co-exist.

Among God's people, adults and children, we allow what we say to each other to touch and affect our perceptions, our attitudes, our plans and our future. As we live our life with God and receive one another in love, our fellowship as his people becomes our roots and our foundation.

A SENSE OF PERSONHOOD IS RECEIVED

The child's sense of identity is something she receives. We each know something of our identity, of who we are, by what we have experienced. A sense of identity, coming through experience, is gradually and consistently offered to us by other persons.

In *The Child, the Family and the Outside World*, D. W. Winnicott conveys the picture of a small person who seems to command her own existence. When she opens her eyes a magnificent world appears, full of the most amazing sights and sounds. When she closes them, it's gone. She controls it, apparently. When she wants something she cries loudly, and before long there comes food or warmth or a cuddle – whatever. It seems to be hers to command. The generally comfortable state is actually determined by the mother who listens for and tends to the baby's needs, not by the baby. So one day the mother as a person is recognised, as she makes clear that her want or need is going to affect the baby's demands and their plans. A reciprocal relationship begins.

First there is the warm, close feeling of needs being met. The child feels loved and nourished and cared for. While these feelings continue, there comes the tension that will always be present in relationships. Mother who has received all the baby's needs and demands, begins to present her own thoughts and feelings. What happens in future will take into account Mother's own wants and interests. This is the beginning of a two-way relationship. Step by step, without violating the child, Mother becomes a person. In this relationship are the roots of future love relationships.

Mother has listened; now Baby begins to listen. At first, Mother may just 'think' out loud, and Baby enjoys hearing her voice. Then comes the time when Baby wants something *now* and Mothers says, 'I would like to finish this first.' Baby screams. A one year old knows what she wants and is not at all willing to wait. Mother is a person whose thoughts and feelings have to be more and more valued if Baby is to receive a sense of her own personhood. So Baby waits.

For mother and baby to continue to develop reciprocal love there will be conversation, the tool for negotiating between people's personal needs and wants. The mother will carefully talk with her child, and sort through what each has presented, and make plans. Sometimes only one need will be met, not both. Mother will see to it, however, that neither is greedy or domineering, and that neither is violated.

I know several Mums who have had or are having a hard time with working this way. I found it hard when I did not feel very good about myself to teach my child to negotiate with me. Similarly, it is hard when you love your baby so much you would like her to have everything she wants. I knew I did not have the money to give Jacqueline everything she wanted, but I still hard to work on this because I used to feel very bad about myself, when I could not.

Communication skills are necessary in order to present oneself. Mother and baby may get quite a long way towards meeting a baby's early demands without any language skills, but only language will help both feel like persons. Mother will present herself using touch, gestures, then words.

Through language, the child gradually learns to negotiate with others. For example, she learns not to hit another person, and to ask for a toy, waiting to hear if she may have it rather than just grabbing it from another person.

In the early years, from birth to age three, a child learns most of her language patterns and lots of basic vocabulary. The relationship to mother and father, brothers and sisters will provide the tension that encourages growth in communication.

The patterns for recognition of the personhood of both mother and child will be those the child will use later, as she grows. The ways she learns to listen and be listened to, presenting herself and asking questions, will be repeated and developed in many other relationships.

LIFE FROM GOD

Not only is each child recognised as a person, but also as a person who is loved by God. Thus, a sense of reverence for one another can grow, and an awareness that God comes to us and speaks to us through one another. When that happens as we receive one another, our lives have an integrated wholeness.

Each child is a person before God. God's love and care does not come to us only at the age of communication skills. The child receives and understands a lot before she even thinks of talking. She listens and hears, sensing the feelings more than the words. This can happen between a child and God without words.

How, then, does a child grow to a sense of being a person with God and understand this? With mother, a pattern has been started, of being present to one another. So with God. We listen to him. We hear him speak to us. I hear God speak to me, and something special happens inside me when I know it's for me. I may hear a prophecy or a bible reading that touches me very deeply and I am aware that God has spoken especially to me.

Children can listen with us in this way, and we can help them present themselves to God. At Post Green the children are fully part of our worshipping family, in everyday life as well as in worship services. Every week we have a celebration of the Eucharist in the Community. It is a short service, about an hour, to which we all come, adults and children. The liturgy is informal and easy-going. It is structured in a way that allows for spontaneity, and is short enough for even our smallest child not to be too restless.

Everyone gets involved, sharing testimonies, offering prayers as appropriate. Recently we had a special opportunity to ask for prayer for healing as the bread and wine were administered. Those who served the elements would stop to pray with anyone who asked as they were served. Some adults asked for prayer and some children did the same. One child stopped the servers and said, 'Please can we pray about the train strike? I don't want it to happen.' Then two small brothers asked, 'Please can we pray for our kitten, because it might die.' In receiving bread and wine these children asked for life for their kitten. They knew they could pray; it mattered to God and to them. Through experience, they knew it was good to present themselves to God. Seeing and hearing the testimonies around them, they knew they were involved in a real conversation.

Adults can help children listen when in church or at worship. They can also help them with their prayers and with sharing what they are happy or concerned about.

Christopher wanted to pray but was unsure. Rowena, one of the single adults from his household, was sitting with him, so he asked her to do it for him. And he learned about how to offer his prayer in front of everyone. At home, when a child says she's worried about something, the adult can say, 'Let's pray about that,' and then do so at that point in time. When a child talks about something that shows God's goodness, tell her you see God at work in her story. As these testimonies are later received by others, the personhood in relationship to God is affirmed.

At the testimony or sharing time in worship, those leading pay direct attention to each person as she offers, receiving the feelings, listening carefully. Sometimes worship touches people deeply, making them cry. We can receive such people, for instance by putting an arm around them. All kinds of feelings can be expressed and received.

When a child speaks, the wording is sometimes funny. Adults can become a bit embarassed, and often they laugh. The child can feel very hurt; what she was sharing was not meant to be funny but serious. She neither feels understood nor received because of the laughter.

Have you ever tried to keep an average two year old listening during a church service? How can you start? It is easier to begin outside church. I remember a conversation Lorna and I had about this when Matthew was two and a half. He seemed determined to fight every attempt she made to encourage him to listen to others. Often he stopped her involvement as well.

'Is there any other time during the week when you can require him to listen to others, when it will not be so difficult if he throws a tantrum in response?'

It is easy, even a relief, to let an energetic two year old leave the table the moment he has finished eating. But at home, keeping Matthew at the table with everyone for a little longer, so he learned to listen in conversation as well as speak, helped him learn that there were times to be quiet.

Recognising God's love for each of us and respecting the life in each person, we will listen very carefully to everyone. As we receive one another's thoughts and feelings we receive the Lord. In this way we feel alive and this is communicated in the words, the music, the bread and wine – the actual ingredients of our worship.

We know the reality of God as we allow all that happens in worship to touch our everyday lives. As we realise the loneliness of others, we allow that loneliness to affect our plans. For instance, we may invite them to spend time in our home. As we really receive another person's thoughts and feelings, they touch our lives, and God will speak to us about offering something to one another. As we are open in listening to and receiving God, he himself will be there with us, through all who are present, including the children.

In participation in the activities of worship we tell God how we feel. Music touches and expresses feelings very deeply, so songs are important, songs that are an expression of every part of us. As the excitement of the music touches us deeply, we respond with excitement. We move toward God and feel befriended and met by him. We have presented ourselves to him. The words enable us to present our thoughts and our understanding as well as our feelings.

As the reciprocal, two-way relationship with God grows, we grow. As we are enabled to take part with the whole of ourselves, we listen and understand new things about God. As we reflect on this together, our lives are changed. The more we are aware of being with God in this listening, receiving way, the more we grow. And our children grow as we enable them to take part with us. Individually and as a church, our relationship to God becomes creative.

In reflecting on your own relationship to children the following may be helpful: Plan to spend time with one child. You could go for a walk, do something together, or just sit down and talk together. Then consider how each of you listened and received the other person.

Section Two

GROWING

Chapter 3
FREEDOM AND RESPONSIBILITY

When I am grown to man's estate
I shall be very proud and great,
And tell the other girls and boys
Not to meddle with my toys.

Robert Louis Stevenson

Freedom and responsibility go hand in hand at one end of the scale, while dependence and powerlessness are at the other. In being fully free, a person is fully responsible for himself in relationship to all other persons with whom he has contact. In knowing himself, a person will realise that no external circumstance really controls this responsibility. Before reaching maturity a person will require certain elements of the environment to be favourable for him to function in a balanced way.

A child, being immature, needs certain input from adults in order to live in a balanced way, appropriate to his growth, his development and safety. He needs help in decisions and in communications and requires encouragement, opportunity. He is always, however, growing towards being able to manage himself independently. Some people will always need the input of others in order to live a balanced life, e.g. handicapped or damaged persons. And every family needs encouraging support from outside.

The baby has no sense of who he is. Not even knowing the sounds that constitute his own name, he is totally dependent on others for his identity.

In the bible, a name was not only a convenient label but something descriptive of a whole identity. In giving the child a name, the church and the parents are giving affirmation at an experiential level of the child's personhood before God. How hard it is to care for the nameless, or the nameless to feel cared for! There are in the world a number of people who, through various political accidents and irregularities, are separated from family, community and country. They almost become objects rather than people, or 'lost souls', like a number of refugees.

In giving a child a name, a family is beginning to help him grow through knowing a secure context and identity. The lost child, who loses his parents either physically or emotionally, loses his sense of identity. He may seem withdrawn, as if lost among the crowd, finding no safe place. In every case, the utter bewilderment of belonging nowhere and to no one produces drastic disorientation. The dependent child needs caring adults who take responsibility for his belonging to them. They will watch and keep up with him, they will set limits against straying too far.

Physical care gives food and warmth, time to sleep, affection, help. It also gives protection and opportunity for growth towards physical independence. At the appropriate time a small child learns to feed himself, to take himself to the toilet. Later he learns to cross roads, ride a bike, take himself to school.

A very young baby does not cry for the fun of it. A crying baby is registering a need he cannot meet for himself. He needs help, and cuddles are reassuring. If he feels insecure, crying alone in a cot or pram does not help; but a caring adult holding him does. Nor are a baby's physical needs fixed by external schedules. Sticking to them come what may and, for instance, not feeding him when he is hungry does not do much for the young baby at all.

Emotional care from the parents and church includes affection and involvement, love and tenderness, which affirm God's attitude to the child. People enjoy his company and want him close. They will hold the baby when he cries and enjoy laughing together. They will understand the strength of baby's sorrow and anger and receive him unquestioningly. This child does not grow up full of insecurity or self-rejection, attitudes which always limit personal growth, since they push the person into basing his decisions on personal needs.

LANGUAGE

Growth in contact with all that is around a person requires communication and negotiation with others. Recognition of myself comes through my having an opportunity to converse with others. The child needs language skills. As soon as he begins to talk he needs conversation, and he needs an environment that facilitates his presenting his thoughts and feelings.

Learning to talk, for a child, is first a question of hearing and listening. Someone talks to him often enough for the baby to realise that those words carry and reflect his parents' attitude to him, their plans for him, their own ideas, thoughts and feelings. Talk to your baby, explain what you are doing, tell him how you think of him, including how much you enjoy his being with you. Tell him that his dirty nappy smells a lot, or that you know how hungry he is. Have an ongoing, even if onesided, conversation.

When Jacqueline was tiny, we had each other for company and I talked to her a lot. I look back now and realise what an asset to her growth our companionship was.

As he reaches nine months or more the baby realises that he can control his mouth and lips to produce sounds like those his family uses. As he does this, it is not helpful for you to change your words to 'baby talk', because the baby is trying to imitate your sounds to learn to speak clearly, not the other way around.

By eighteen months, many children are joining the words together into small sentences. It is time to concentrate on conversation. In communication, the child is now trying to negotiate with others, and failing to sort things out because of his limited talking skills he may have terrible tantrums. (These may also be caused by his believing that everyone should do as he says and being equally unable to understand, with his limited language skills, that they are not going to, and ending up very frustrated with words.)

Justin seemed to get very frustrated with all of us. He was coming up to two and often got very angry.

'What are we going to do?' we asked ourselves after yet another disastrous mealtime.

'He seems so frustrated with everything I don't even know if he understands what we say to him,' said Sylvia, his mother.

We talked together and decided that Justin was frustrated both in understanding us and being understood.

'How do we hurry this stage along?' Jon, Justin's father, questioned.

'I suppose we could make very sure that we talk to him a lot,' I offered.

It seemed a good suggestion.

I added, 'I would like to sit next to Justin every mealtime and make sure that we have lots of conversation together.'

That is what we did. Justin grew quite quickly into a stage

35

of lots of talking and lots of questions, a very sociable child.

If the toddler is a second or later child, busy parents may find that his growing independence has left them freer for chores, but they are spending less time in conversation now when he needs it so much. It may not be possible to stop and talk every time your child wants to, but look for opportunities, such as while you are on the bus or in the car, even while you are at the table at the end of a meal, while he is on his potty or in the bath. Make these talking times.

Children learn vocabulary through listening. They learn the patterns of conversation through listening, and they learn skills in using these through practice. So if a child is going to grow in understanding himself through communication, how will he learn to present himself? First, others will use words with him. Not simply a word list, or even just labelling his feelings, but by telling him their own so that he can experience them. Notice that parents normally seem to feel obliged not to tell their children how they feel. It is vital that I say when I am excited, sad, worried, discouraged or even angry. Those moods that surround either parent are recognised by the child intuitively. If we name them, putting them into words, our children can see how adults manage their feelings, learning two things at the same time.

BEING IN CHARGE OF ONESELF

First he will learn the names of feelings. Then he will learn how to be in charge of himself without having to deny or repress his feelings. For example, he will learn how to be angry without hurting others; how to be sad, without making others run around him to make him feel differently; how to be irritable when he is depressed and apologise sincerely afterwards when he sees how his mood hurt others.

Five-year-old Christopher came home from school every day saying he would never go again. 'But you have to,' Lorna would say. Both were discouraged with the struggle of convincing him that school was both essential and obligatory. Then, for a while, she made a special point of listening hard to what Christopher was saying and receiving his feelings.

'I hate school. I am never going again, I hate school.'

'You hate school.'

'Yes, I hate it. I am going to stay at home with you and Matthew.'

'You would like to stay here.'

'I don't like school; it's noisy and everyone pushes.'

'You don't like being pushed.'

He had pulled off his coat and was disappearing upstairs.

'No. Mum, can I have a drink of orange?'

As Christopher was able to come home and express his tiredness, frustration, sadness or whatever he felt that day, things changed. A few minutes of Mum's finding out and helping with feelings released the inner tension of bottled up un-named feelings. Gradually the statements about school changed, while Lorna had done nothing apart from listening actively.

Thoughts are probably easier to put into words. Remember again that a child's planning skills can be helped by being with you as you plan. Similarly, as you work out plans as a family, listening to each other's ideas, reflecting together afterwards, the child learns through experience the principles of corporate decision-making.

Jacqueline was nearly six; we were getting ready to go to help at a children's camp.

'Packing is such a chore,' I sighed.

'I want to pack my own case.'

'Alright. I'll give you the clothes to put in.'

'No. I want to do it all myself.'

She was very determined, yet I knew that many things could get left out.

'Well, why don't you make a list of all the things you need and collect them together. Then I will look over it to see if I can think of any more things you may want while we are away.'

She pondered.

'Why don't I make a list and show you before I collect everything and pack it. Then I will tick each thing when I get it.' (We had made lists together before.)

Two or three years further on I gave up checking her packing lists and received only occasional questions and comments.

'Mum, shall I take all my socks, or just one or two pairs?'

'I don't think I'll take a separate case for Peter Teddy this year. He can share mine.' (Peter Teddy had his own special toy case that had been my sister's years before.)

Single parents of one or two children often tell thoughts and feelings to their children more than in a two-parent family. But watch out! The child must also experience adults telling each other thoughts and feelings, making plans and so on. The single parent can take the child or children to visit other families with him, so that this pattern is opened to them. Similarly, in the case of the single parent sharing thoughts and feelings with his children, it is easy to put the kind of emotional pressure on a child that only another adult is really able to stand.

People, both adults and children, often have different ways of seeing reality. It may come down to one seeing something very objectively while the other responds subjectively. Both are real and acceptable ways of seeing reality. Unless both people really work at dialogue, careful listening and acknowledging of differences, the result may well be argument.

THE WORLD AROUND US

Growing up toward freedom and responsibility takes us into experiencing our thoughts, feelings and ideas in the context of the world around us.

The five to ten year olds live in a world of curiosity, adventure and challenge. More about these in later chapters; here it is enough to mention that they are involved in growth in responsibility. A new decision which does not work out as planned, may make even a playing child feel guilty. This is a good/bad value judgment which hampers growth, and it is better to introduce the thought, 'Now, if I were to try this again, what would I do differently?' In this way, the child begins to look back and consider other possibilities and alternatives. Why did this project not work as planned? Guilt and condemnation cause a person to repress considerations of the project and leave it untouched, without learning.

A child's learning to think back constructively comes from shared *reflection*, or thinking over. The adult can ask his own questions, share his own thoughts as plans don't work out as anticipated. 'Why did it not work this time, when it did last time?' Most important of all is to know the child's activities and projects, and be able to draw from him reflection on their effectiveness and his feelings about it. Reflection is not a time for pushing a child into adult attitudes and approaches. It is a time for helping him reflect and offering him an opportunity to follow through his own thoughts.

This may relate to activities that involve things or those that involve other people. A child will try things out, constructing with wood or boxes or whatever, and he will discover limitations, but he learns most by reflecting on the effectiveness of what he has done. Was the result what he expected, what he wanted? What might he change, and how? That opens his mind to consider creative solutions.

A child will play with words and then with communication. Not long after I started school I wandered home by myself, reflecting, talking to myself about the day and considering it. By the time I reached my house, I was reflecting out loud on some 'naughty' words I had heard. As I repeated them in a sing-song kind of way I realised I could be heard by my mother – the kitchen window was wide open. She was aware that I knew she had heard. As I went in the door she asked, 'What were you saying?' 'Oh nothing,' I said, not wanting to share *this* experimenting and reflection. I cannot remember being punished or even challenged, and I never really got into the habit of swearing. Having tried it, it never seemed quite what I wanted to do. Probably the biggest factor in that was that my parents did not swear. (In some families swear words are used like adjectives, so we must not be critical of children for whom they are family words.)

Relationships seem harder to reflect on, probably because we adults are liable to put things, words and achievements before persons, and so are not always very good with our social skills. It can be easier to snub or ignore someone than to really sort out our differences with him. This is to reject the other person, and is as destructive to him as abuse or physical violence. So how do we begin to help our child to handle his difficulties with his friends?

Last year, at one of Post Green's teaching camps, I was sitting in a friend's caravan chatting, when we heard a great wailing outside.

'Mummy, Matthew will never play with me again. I *know* he won't.'

'Well, Hannah, tell me about it.'

'I'm so sad, and Matthew is sad, too.'

'Can you tell me what happened?'

'He was swinging his bat and hit me by mistake. And I ran away crying.'

'Oh, dear.'

'He didn't know I knew it was an accident.' The wails by now were less pronounced, more like big sobs.

'He won't play with me any more.'

'Do you think it might help if you told him you were sorry you just ran away?'

'I don't know.'

'Would you like me to come with you when you say it?'

Across the field Matthew was now recovering from his tears and saying,

'I ran away. I bet Hannah won't want to play with me anymore.'

It was not too difficult to help them.

FANTASY AND REALITY

Once a child starts school, he is beginning to grapple with the difference between fantasy and reality. As I experience doing something concrete, either in the shape of a project or a relationship or in communication, I am working in reality. What I anticipated, thought of, dreamt up; whatever I thought the activity might be like, was fantasy. Our interaction and involvement with people and experience of things is reality. As an adult, I normally know the difference, but a child often does not.

A lot of disappointments and frustrations in life stem from the fact that the gap between fantasy and reality is too big.

We have a strong imagination, a clear fantasy of what will happen. It is crucial that each person has enough positive experiences of life to be happy to live with reality. We must not lose fantasy; dreams and aspirations are necessary to all of us. We must, however, find a way to integrate them with the world around us: our ambitions with our real skills and abilities, our romantic dreams with the real person next to us, our inventions with the reality of the tools and materials we have.

Every time we find ourselves saying, 'If only I had done . . .', we are recalling fantasy as opposed to reality. At this point, it is time for reflection and a conclusion that says, 'If I had the same circumstances again I would. . . .' This allows our very positive imaginings to touch reality and be integrated.

Most children before school age do not differentiate fantasy from reality. There are several stages that precede the ability to integrate these two. A child in the lounge will not realise that you in the kitchen cannot see what he sees. While watching TV, he will ask, 'Why did the man do that?' Then one day he realises that you cannot see round corners, that you are not really seeing reality through his eyes but your own. 'Come and see this. You really must come in here and see.'

One of my daughter's favourite stories was a bit frightening, but she always chose it for bedtime, till one day she realised the story was fixed in the words of the book. It would always have a happy ending. Her fantasy had had room for a fear that one day the ending might be bad. The small child does not recognise the unchanging aspects of reality. The wolf might eat Red Riding Hood this time.

Think back together on things that have happened in the day, on major and minor activities and events. Reflect on feelings that were responses to these and on times when you were not together. Such reflection is time for each person to consider reality for themselves, not for the adult to teach the child reality, or fantasy will simply be repressed. Reflection facilitates integration. The child will then also reflect on his own. His sitting silent or even talking to himself is how he will begin to work on his skill in integrating and reflecting constructively.

It is impossible for him, however, to fully integrate fantasy and reality if he always does his reflecting alone. This is true, incidentally, of both adults and children. Left totally to our own thinking, we can easily get reflecting and fantasy mixed up.

MAKING DECISIONS

Opportunity to make decisions helps the child grow towards maturity in dealing with reality, rather than just day-dreaming. This has two aspects. There are decisions that affect only me, e.g. how I spend my time, what I want to play with and so on. Then there are decisions that relate to the family or the church.

The child who is seven-plus should have frequent opportunity both for personal decisions that affect life and for play. A few years ago I took a group of eight to ten year olds camping. They were responsible for everything they possibly could be. I was a kind of back-up person, adviser if asked, the one who set limits against any really dangerous activity. (I also found myself helping them sort out a very few conflicts.) The children chose their menus, did the cooking, decided what, how and when to eat. They decided when to go to bed and when to get up.

This was an exciting adventure, for each normally lived in a world where most of this was decided by the others in the family.

41

They did what everyone else did. They did not consider they could seriously question the system, apart from throwing the occasional rebellious tantrum. On the first evening one girl came to me: 'Should I go and have a wash now before I go to bed?' I was expected and 'supposed' to say, 'Yes.' Instead I said, 'It's up to you.' Here, suddenly, was a child who could make a decision about whether to wash! She consulted her friends. After some deliberation they all decided to wash.

They grew immediately in their sense of freedom and responsibility. I had given them the environment, opportunity and encouragement. One boy had decided not to get himself breakfast before our outing, or make a packed lunch. He was absolutely ravenous before he solved his problem. But he had had a real choice and responsibility.

At home, this pattern of growth begins with toys or pocket money which belongs to the children and over which they have complete control. As children grow, they must become involved in family decisions, about mealtimes, chores, and other corporate aspects of life. They learn to talk and plan, adults and children together.

As my daughter has grown into areas of responsibility and decision-making, I have found myself concentrating on various aspects of life. Sometimes my fear has made me want to limit her, to stop her growth. Instead, I have learned to give her responsibility while at the same time making sure she is equipped with the skills and information necessary. An example would be how to deal with tickets, trains, timetables, inquiries. On her first trip to shop in London alone, I was excited and worried, but I managed to keep my advice more practical than controlling or manipulative. 'Well, if you get on the train and you're afraid it's the wrong one, ask another passenger.' 'A ticket collector will happily direct you to your platform, or try looking it up on the departures board.' Sometimes it has been very much more difficult for me, but now she is a responsible older teenager we can talk about her projects in a real dialogue. Without hidden controls on my side or rebellion on hers, my experience helps in seeing the pitfalls or realities of a project. We have reached the stage of adult to adult communication.

FRIENDSHIP WITH ADULTS

Let us consider a child who has learned to take responsibility for himself, and has a growing and significant involvement in family decisions. He knows what he thinks, how his decisions affect others and he makes his own choice. At this stage of maturity all each of us needs is friendship, peer friendship. Someone to whom one can say, 'I know what I think, I know what I feel, I see the possible choices. Let me hear what you think as well; then I will decide.'

In the world of church life, if we are going to grow into freedom and responsibility, there must at all these stages be similar opportunities. All ages must have access to conversation, to real experiences and reflection together and growing responsibilities for themselves in the life of the church. The common pattern of priest and people can deny the personhood, the development to maturity of each individual, adult or child.

With interaction and sharing, I get a better picture of reality. On my own, I may be confused by my fears and fantasies. But you must not direct me, because if you do, that makes you responsible for my choices, and I stay a child. We can be of mutual help, in talking things over. Then I can decide for myself.

Knowing whatever I think and feel and knowing the circumstances, I make my own choice. But that freedom does not mean that I expect to get everything I want, or that what I choose will be comfortable to me. When I make a responsible choice, however, and its consequences include what is unpleasant, there is no one else I can blame. It was my choice.

Jesus was free in his choice to die. He knew his thoughts and feelings: I will do what my Father tells me. He deeply felt the agony of Gethsemane, both personal pain and sorrow for his disciples. Being fully aware of all this, he still chose to continue and die. He might have chosen to back out; it would have felt more comfortable. It was a real choice; he was not manipulated or controlled. This was maturity.

I sometimes have chosen, and probably will again, to follow a course of action that feels too hard or distressing or uncomfortable. Freedom does not mean the absence of hardship. It means I know I have made my own decision.

If I share with you how I have experienced God, I can allow you to reflect with me. You might add, 'Now, I experience God a little differently. . . .' Because we seek God in our quietness, alone, inside ourselves, we may each be sharing our fantasy and not the true nature of God. Inside each of us there is not only God but also the patterns of the world, our imagination and experience, our intuitions and perceptions. To understand the true nature of God, we must have adult friendship; 'soul friendship' to know ourselves free and responsible in relation to him. So, too, do our children. Reflection with them in personal, family or church worship is a way to begin to work on this.

POWERLESSNESS FROM FEAR

The opposite of 'freedom' is 'powerlessness', as seen in the child who had no idea that a possible choice might be not to make a packed lunch. He had no sense of involvement in the decision-making of his family's life. Everything pushed him along, he was just a thing, a mechanical train on someone else's track. Rather, he should be helped to grow up knowing his own responsibility for himself in relation to others.

Similarly, when fear controls us there seem to be no choices, and fear can sometimes be based on fantasy. If we balance our fear against our experience we can begin to see there really is a choice. If, however, we live in an oppressive situation, whether family or state, we may have experienced that there are factors which actually bar our discovering the fullness of personhood as responsible people.

One child I know enjoyed playing the recorder. On moving to a new school, other children threatened to beat her up if she joined the recorder group. Immature, she saw no choice; she immediately stopped playing and felt very hurt about it.

Reflection is key to growth, but the environment for its growth cannot include control, manipulation, punishment or rejection.

Consider some ways your child has, or does not have, responsibility and choice; for example, on what to spend pocket money, what to wear, how to play.

Consider the next six months to a year. What responsibility will your child grow into coping with during this year? How can you prepare him for greater responsibility?

Chapter 4
CREATION AND CREATIVITY

At the Seaside

When I was down beside the sea
A wooden spade they gave to me
    To dig the sandy shore.
My holes were empty like a cup
In every hole the sea came up
    Till it could come no more.

Robert Louis Stevenson

Creativity exists in every person; it is something that is alive, organic, growing from within the person. It does not find expression simply in using the arts in worship services, but rather as something that is alive in us as a gift from God, part of each human being he created.

The foundation for creativity lies in the identity of each person and in the affirming of it in one another. It is then nurtured, watered and cared for, and grown to maturity. As suggested in *The Child in the Church*, a British Council of Churches publication, 'What we pass on to our children is not the painting but the paint box.' Underlying the nurture of each person's life is the attitude of the one who provides the paintbox, giving all that is necessary for a person to live and express all of herself and her giftedness.

What is needed is opportunity, materials and an affirming environment. Then we see the fruit of the child's creativity. It is hers to consider and value for herself. The buying and selling of art or music, artistic professionalism, the comparison of skills, are not very relevant to this creativity. God is interested in the person, not an 'objective' evaluation. The fruit of creativity in a mature adult may well be highly valued by others, as when a person is creative in her use of science. That which is the fruit of external pressures and controls, whose expression is, for example, so determined by commercial or other social pressure that the designer no longer feels it is hers, is not reflective of God's creativity.

When we look at a child's creative work, we can see, with appreciative eyes, her enjoyment, her expression, her own presentation of herself. When we show interest and affirm both what she does and who she is, the child has room to grow.

The children I meet seem to have a sense of wonder and awe that is not so apparent in adults. It is the wonder of life around us. Once processed by society we seldom stop and stare, to reflect on creation or to see and experience new things with freshness and wonder. My grown-up, 'scientific' mind evaluates function, purpose, productivity, usefulness, commercial value. The mystery, the wonder that is present regardless of these material values is almost lost. Not so in children.

The wonder of childhood in new experiences, in curiosity, is unchannelled by the values of society, and so has a freshness that I find only too easy to brush aside. The child who feels the touch and pull of the wind stands delighted next to me, while my racing mind, considering its potential damage, is concerned about damage to local property. But the child is enjoying the wind with all her senses.

I find I must approach each child with some humility and reverence for this sense of wonder. For wonder and a sense of the mysteries of life are strong elements in wholeness in worship.

When I see a baby beginning the discovery of her environment, I look around at how she is experiencing it. A new baby's senses are very alert; how can I encourage her excitement and joy?

What is she hearing? No sounds are programmed out as irrelevant, for selective listening only develops with experience. So she hears the clock, the door, a voice, the weather, animals, birds, vehicles. To find the source of each sound, I have to disengage my own selective mechanisms to introduce her to the sound she hears. The sound of a vehicle, the knock at the door, the sound of a different voice, the chink of bottles, the clunk of the fridge door . . ., all are pictures of life going on.

Once we have lived with a smell for a short while we cease to notice it consciously. But what are the new or familiar smells a child is experiencing; am I alert to them? Familiar perfume may bring baby's mum to mind. There are food smells that suggest mealtime, and a variety of bathroom smells. Outside there are traffic smells of many kinds, smells of trees and grass and wood and smoke. How many new 'smell' experiences does my child have between home and shops or church? Do I notice them and talk about them?

Babies and small children have a highly active sense of taste. Hence their reaction against strong-tasting foods. Alertness to the experience of life includes experiencing lots of flavours, lots of textures, a taste of what is bitter and of what is sweet, of chewy and smooth.

Within the limits of safety, the child who crawls or is barefoot outside will be aware of the textures of stone, of grass, of sand and earth, leaves or gravel. After the smoothness of baby's clothes and sheets the child experiences being touched and held. Water slops around her at bath time and waving feet and hands drop surprising splashes on her face. I watched with interest as my friend laid her small baby right down in the bath water. That her ears might get full of water did not bother Lisa; she seemed much more able to enjoy the water around her.

Why do babies so often wear pastel shades of pink or blue, or even white? These colours seem much more reflective of an adult impression of purity and innocence than of the child's discovery of life. How much more exciting if when Baby lies on her back, waving her feet, she sees glimpses of red and yellow instead of just another shade of white. And above is not just a white ceiling, but a coloured mobile that bobs and dips and flutters. How many times I put Jacqueline's pram near a tree for her to sleep. The clouds sailed by, and she was fascinated for ages by the fluttering of the leaves against the light of the sky.

When I realised the significance of colour I began to reconsider the clothes I wore when with children. In craft workshops it is easy to choose old jeans and serviceable, yet sombre, smocks or shirts. What about my favourite bright colours?

CURIOSITY

At first, life seems to be a kaleidoscope of sense experiences. Sometimes a pattern appears and goes again. But then the baby's curiosity comes into its own as she becomes aware of her own physical identity and of her own growing ability to co-ordinate

47

movements, to direct those waving arms and legs or turn her head.

The image of life suddenly takes new form as she can grab or hold on to something to try its taste or touch in her mouth. She can watch the colour she is passing. Her discovery of life becomes an aspect that is increasingly determined by her own interest. Life is still a continuing experience of trying, selecting an ever-widening range of new experiences, remembering what is *special* in each.

This growth is the opposite of limiting. The objective, scientific element in me wants to say about each experience, 'Remember what is relevant in each.' But the word 'relevant' suggests a functional valuing. The taste of a Marmite sandwich to me has nothing to do with function; I enjoy the taste for itself, so I remember it for that. The feel of the sun on my face, or the sound of the waves rolling the pebbles down the beach is thrilling. The colours of the evening sky make my sense of wonder grow larger inside me, as well as my reverence and worship of God.

Nor is this experience of all that exists around me purely aesthetic. It does include the discovery of ways and means, of structures and plans, of principles. Through these comes a sense of being in charge of aspects of our environment, like making the bricks stand tall like a tower, as I want, or determining where I go on my bike, through learning to pedal and steer. These are functional aspects of discovery.

I also discover limitations of identity and environment, like the fact that I cannot fly, but I can jump a little. Can I make water stay in my bucket when I turn it over? Can I . . . can I . . .? 'What are the limits?' asks the curious child.

PLAY IS WHAT IT IS ALL ABOUT

There is the discovery of what will do what, and how. What can I do and how will I do it? As I grow, the limits become wider. The child plays with the concrete or the mysterious aspects of life, to analyse them in a kind of scientific discovery. What happens if I put my hankie in the bath water? Where does the water go when I pull out the plug? And why does it go? Why don't my toys move of their own accord like animals or people? Can I make them move? It is an endless stream of questions and possibilities. So many times the question 'Why?' seems tedious to the parent of a three year old, but it is the substance of life for the child.

Activities like painting and story-telling allow each child to follow her imagination. This means that there is no scientific objective or conclusion that has to be formulated. The child's imagination can take her where she wants. Whatever colours she wishes can be painted together, whatever notes she wants can be played together. There does not even have to be a plan before she starts. Young children equipped with paint do not usually try to make their creations symbolic or representative of anything. The experience is what counts.

Play can also be a copy of the life of the family or group of which the child is part, a sort of rehearsing. The tea party or dressing up, mothers and fathers, hospital, school, church or other social events are played over as children observe and imitate the forms in an attempt to master them, to become part of the life of society.

MATERIALS, FRIENDSHIP AND ENVIRONMENT

The environment can encourage discovery. Even a tidy garden can have a corner for a sandpit, or a place where water can be poured for mudpies or clay. I found our house could be tidied again after play, and schedules could be allowed to slip a bit when Jacqueline wanted to play just a little longer in the bath. The neatness, order or detail that the adult had chosen gave way to provide opportunity for the creative growth of another person.

Materials can come from all sorts of places, free. Jacqueline had a collection of empty pots and plastic containers that were our alternative to buying toys for the sandpit. They cost me nothing and worked perfectly.

Playing with sound can involve banging or shouting, whispering or tapping. There are the saucepans, empty tins and boxes to bang, stones to be poured into plastic tubs, and so on. Musical instruments, too, can be very home made. Jacqueline and I experimented not just with a cut out shape, like a toy guitar, but the kinds of instruments that we found in the *Musical Instruments Recipe Book* (E. Romney, Penguin). We listened and made all kinds of music through discovery, and enjoyed those simple, rambling songs that young children make up themselves.

Construction is done with the aid of empty containers, boxes, tubes, fabric scraps and general bric-a-brac, as well as with kits such as Lego or Tinker-Toy. In my work with older children, eight to eleven, I have found that they are as much challenged and more creative with miscellaneous scraps than with whatever formal materials we provide.

Paint, like clay, is essential. Both have properties that encourage expression of both feeling and form.

Finger paints and other material can be used before using brushes or 'proper' tools. A child discovers for herself that she might want to make a particular form, e.g. draw a person. It is an adult concept that, faced with a painting, says, 'What is it?' It probably is not anything particular; it is an experience.

Children explore the neighbourhood, the walls and trees, the slopes and gulleys. They hide and jump and roll. If furniture cannot be climbed on, and there is no climbing frame, find outside walls and steps and playgrounds.

We go on expeditions with our children, walking among hills and woodland. Children do not mind if the weather is poor; walking in the rain means puddles and splashes and the feel of rain on our faces. Children also enjoy a chance to experience animals at close quarters. If you are not too keen on keeping pets yourself, find fellow church members with dogs or cats to visit and spend time with. Understanding animals is not a purely scientific experience but also tactile. And what does a cat look like when it yawns or eats or walks around?

I have collected a box of old clothes for dressing up and a variety of makeup. Small children will not normally be doing drama for presentation as they play, for they see the world only through their own eyes. They are trying themselves out in various roles and do not get involved in how another person feels until they reach seven-plus. Puppets are fun, too, as children play with the social patterns they see.

Where is the adult or parent while the child is doing so much discovery? We are the listeners and the encouragers. When our child rushes in to say, 'Guess what I've found, come and see!', the child's sense of curiosity and discovery is affirmed if we go. If we do not, she wanders off, concluding, 'Well, what I discover really cannot be very important after all. It is nothing, really.' If I cannot go at that moment, I try to find a way to assure her of my interest anyway, and then go as soon as I can. Often children's eyes see the world in ways that are new to me. When I am with them, I try to be a follower, a learner, for a while.

Important, too, is an opportunity for children to be and play with other children who are making similar or complementary discoveries. This is helpful in a way that parents cannot be. Play group or some similar group is a useful asset.

CHALLENGE

The challenge to go beyond what has already been discovered or experienced brings continued growth. It is a pushing out of the limits of past experience. Many adults have lost their desire to rise to a challenge, or apparently so, yet they can see its effect on others. Some sports encourage people to challenge themselves, not primarily to win over others, but to do what they set out to do. Educational structures of programmed learning proceed with small steps; each is an attainable but challenging goal for the learner.

The child of school age also seeks challenge. She challenges herself, setting goals and working toward them. Self-imposed challenges can be in areas of no interest to anyone else. I remember as a child setting myself to count all the way to 1000. And my memory was jogged by overhearing my friend Christopher counting up in much the same way. We were both challenging ourselves with numbers.

In all areas where there is new experience there can be challenge. 'I can ride a trike; can I ride a two-wheeler?' 'You can jump; can you hop or skip?' 'Can you play two-balls or skip with a rope?' Within a family, challenge gives lots of potential for growth in areas not offered by school. Schools, even the best, are involved in an essential processing, but its whole structure sets limits which keep it within geographical, subject and financial limitations.

The family in the church is an ideal environment for challenge, with new people and different people. The interests and hobbies of others provide challenge for the inquisitive minds and lives of our children. Alexander, my twelve-year-old friend, spends a lot of time with Robert King, who is an adult. They keep bees together.

As a family or church, tackle walking or climbing together, swimming or other such activities. As a group, learn sailing or canoeing or even abseiling. Visit others whose lifestyle is different; visit and understand. Go on holiday to a new environment: a farm or village, a town or city. Try the foods of other cultures.

Many children, because it is inconvenient, never really experience different kinds of travel. What about going by bus, and learning to go alone? Or by train? One of my daughter's sixteen-year-old friends had never travelled by train or underground, or gone further than ten miles from home without her parents. They never thought about it as a new experience to be tackled, though they are very caring parents. One of my friends realised that first her parents and later her husband had always taken care of all travel arrangements, even buying the tickets. So she was amazed by the experience of travelling alone to Scotland. It gave a new perspective on family patterns and routines. These must not be allowed to cover up or deny opportunity for challenge and achievement.

It is obvious that a child's challenges might take her into situations she could not cope with or even into danger. The family and church environment offers challenge, but with protection. Through children and adults doing new activities together the children learn safe routines – everything from reading enclosed instructions to listening to the leader. We talk about what we are experiencing together so that my own and the children's perceptions can be shared. Some examples:

'Why don't we go that way?'

'I think because the sign said. . . .'

'Let's ask, anyway.'

This gives the child the chance to lead and me to follow, which in turn gives me a chance to see how safety conscious she is. For instance, a child begins to ride a bike on the road. An adult should go, too. Then when the child reaches the stage of going alone, she has confidence in her ability.

The majority of challenges that a child would choose to tackle for herself probably will not have a dangerous element. Having time to chat with her as she comes and goes will also encourage her to keep us informed about her plans.

Sometimes, however, the danger is there, though less obvious. Accidents at home are far more likely than, for instance, on the road. As we decide to offer our child gradually more opportunity around the house – cooking, carpentering, wiring a plug and so on – we can check they use materials wisely and avoid accidents. Awareness of potential dangers can help parents keep children safe. For example, when a very small child wants to tackle climbing the stairs, we first teach her to come down safely.

When I worked on crafts with our children at our Summer Camps I realised how frustrating it is to work with scissors that are so safe they won't cut. I have now changed them all over for ones that will cut quite well. So we cut out things with good scissors; they do the job and don't hurt much. We learn with a small hammer, not a big one, and a serrated knife that is efficient.

In a carefully planned way, enable your child to tackle her own challenges about school and getting there. Do not be too protective. Let her find her own ways to save or spend with small amounts while she is young, or she will not be able to handle bigger decisions well, as the amount of money she handles gets larger as she grows older. Let her try.

'I want to be in the band at school.' Trying out this new challenge may involve talking to a teacher, learning more about playing an instrument and much later playing in the band. Experiments with sounds and music find expression in rhythms and forms the children play together.

It might be helpful to note that the trust which enables you to let your child tackle new things alone comes gradually. When correcting your child, encourage her to come back to you to talk if she really cannot stick to what you require, or does not understand. If you discipline through punishment when the child has not obeyed you blindly (though this kind of punishment may sometimes have a place), your child will try, and manage, to keep some of her activity secret from you. The coming back to you does not necessarily imply that you will change your decision, but will rather help the child know that she can talk with you about her questions and doubts and difficulties, and share with you the pressure of not being allowed to do what all her friends seem to be doing. Then her tackling of new challenges will not be mixed up with a fight for identity. When the right to have a say seems, to the child, to be denied, she may tackle new things in direct defiance of you. It is better to learn to talk and negotiate before this stage is reached. Try to avoid new challenges becoming the arena of a battle of wills, for this works against safety. If you must have a battle of wills, and all of us do, it is best to find another time and place for them.

ADVENTURE

There are lots of creative activities that take children beyond

53

the realms of parents. These become adventures, major projects that the child chooses herself and carries through herself. As aspects of growth to the fullest potential, these steps the child must make with the parents staying quite deliberately in the background.

Many adventures in creativity happen in school. 'If I work very hard, I think I can do it. . . .' 'I know I can do it; please let me try.'

Jacqueline wanted to do history so much that she undertook to do it outside lesson time when it would not fit into the timetable alongside her other O-level choices. It was her adventure that she followed through, not mine. And she achieved it by her own effort and her sense of what she could do and wanted to do. Others may challenge themselves to solve problems, to express themselves in art, to play an instrument. Self-knowledge comes as a person realises the truth of her own abilities in the context of the adventures she sets for herself. Some things she will find she cannot do.

The world in which our children are growing up has far greater opportunity for choice and discovery than ever before. Parents can neither teach everything to their child, nor be conversant with all the areas that their child will tackle. Rather, each adult can facilitate the child's knowing her own potential and giftedness, and her knowing how to achieve her own aims realistically and safely. Many times it happens simply in saying, 'How are you going to start?' or, 'What happens if : . .?'

In the coming together of creativity and responsibility, the child discovers what she can do and cope with. In making her own decisions and choices she will find a real identity in her creativity. She will then reach the point of saying, 'I know what I can do and how to do it. And I can cope with the result of my choices.'

This last part, balancing choice and consequence, is critically important. Most of us, and our children, have to earn a living doing work that does not seem creatively fulfilling. This is common to most people today. It would be at least discouraging, if not destructive, to raise our children to think otherwise. Rather, our creativity becomes more a part of our leisure time. Comparatively few people earn their living by doing what pleases them most. Some of the hardness is taken out of more monotonous occupations if the person knows that in her leisure time she can tackle that which challenges her creatively and affirms her natural giftedness.

PRESSURES THAT LIMIT CREATIVITY

Fear is probably the greatest barrier to developing creativity. There is a parent's fear that the child's ability is not enough, or is not normally acceptable, as for instance when a boy wants to learn to dance. Social pressures cause fear in parents and the interest may be stifled. Interests may be unusual, but none the less valid.

Not every child who plays a musical instrument has to reach competition standard. Self expression is not about success or failure, but more about doing what I want to do and enjoying myself.

Comparison to external standards (competition) is destructive of creativity. Comparing standards limits people to presenting themselves in a constricted form, and then having another person pass a value judgment on the level of success or failure. The validity of any creative activity will rest in 'Have I done what I wanted to do in the way I wanted to?'

If your child shows a real interest and aptitude in any particular area, such as art or music, be careful before you push her into this as a career. A career has to match the demands of the market and social pressure. And a very satisfying form of expression can be taken away as the originator has to cut it to fit the demands of others. Make sure your child has lots of different ways to be creative.

I do a lot of hand-knitting, making up designs as I go along. Stripes and motifs, pictures and shapes and lots of colours. I make presents. I am often urged by friends to sell these jumpers commercially. But I hesitate, for most shops or customers say that I must prove originality, or meet deadlines, or this or that, and I am in danger of feeling I can no longer do what I wish with my creativity. So I just carry on with my hobby.

Similarly my taste should not control my response to a child's creativity. The clothes that young teenagers wear are very different from those of the previous generation. And while you were glad your child took to music do not be surprised when she makes different music from what you would prefer. I enjoy the novelty and seeming strangeness of the clothes and hairstyles I see around me. I enjoy seeing and experiencing the life my child is discovering.

Consider and note down your responses to children's expression. Do you feel positive about young people's attitudes where they differ from your own? Or are you unsure, or negative? After reconsidering your notes, find out about the young people's tastes, till you understand and appreciate them, even though your taste is still different.

Chapter 5
RELATIONSHIPS

> I wriggle and I wriggle
> I make quite a fuss,
> But still you love me, Lord.
> Scratch my back
> And give me a hug
> And I'll know you love me more.
>
> **Maggie Durran**

Probably the underlying key to all growth is love. Love received. Many people who have been deprived of love and who are lonely and unhappy, after experiencing even a few moments' love, have spent the rest of their lives trying to find it again. It is better to be loved for a minute than never be loved at all. Once I realised that momentary contact counted as well as spending longer together, I learned to greet children whenever I saw them. A nod, a wave, a 'hello' are all worthwhile. Sometimes I am a bit absent-minded. Usually that is when I am thinking hard about something 'important' or worrying to myself.

It is our love, the adult giving to the child, that waters the seed of life in each person. In an adult–child relationship, the adult consistently gives, the child receives and sometimes gives. By the time he reaches adulthood he will give love to others. The mature person gives love in relationships and receives too, as for instance in a good friendship, in which both parties give. Also, God loves the lonely and deprived and weeps for them. Yet knowledge of his love for them will grow only as they first receive love through others.

God is at the heart of this love and its growth. He first gave us love, and we grew till we could give love. In John's epistle we read, 'We love, because God first loved us.' (1 John 4:19; *RSV*)

Love is the foundation of life. Both before and after birth the baby can receive love that builds life as an individual, as a member of a family and of the church. Without love, his sense of personhood is not positive.

What then are the principles of the love that brings life to children? Firstly, it is not based on the parents' needs. Love gives without needing the other person to give back. If I, as a potential parent, feel that if only I had a baby to smile at me and depend on me, then I would feel loved, or better, my love is probably based on need. To think that a child can help me at this point in my own deprivation is a fantasy and is hurtful to the child. If, in my feeling rejected and depressed, I want someone to make me feel better, a child cannot offer me this.

Enjoy your child for who he is and neither expect or require a return of what you offer him. Receive him joyfully when he laughs with you. But if you demand a smile and feel hurt if he does not give it, he will not want to smile. He is not mature enough to meet your demand.

In telling a child I love him, for who he is, I say something like, 'I am glad you are you. . . . I love you' and 'I enjoy being with you.'

A few months ago I phoned the Lodge to speak to Christopher; he was seven at the time.

'Hello, is that Christopher?'

'Yes.'

'It's Maggie here.'

'Yes, I could tell it was you.'

'Christopher, had you heard that Mike is showing some slides on Antarctica tonight? I wanted to invite you to come with me.'

'You mean me, come with you?'

'Yes. Would you like to?'

'I would. Do you mean it?'

'Yes, I do. I shall enjoy going with you. Shall I bring some popcorn or something?'

'Oh, yes! What time shall we go?'

Our friendship is important to Christopher, and it is exciting to me. I do enjoy his company.

Through our words and actions we offer love to children. When I find myself only managing to be irritable, I stop and examine myself. Now, I recognise that I am irritable when I am tired or not very well. So I take another look at what I plan to do, to give myself a little extra time. I also find that my own inner resources are limited and I need the help and support of the family of

God's people to sustain my love for a child. What I am feeling shows me that God created us to live in a wider, interdependent family, bigger than the basic nuclear family unit.

The love of God is a love that never gives up and never dies. It is secure. 'For I am certain that nothing can separate us from his love: neither death nor life, neither angels nor other heavenly rulers or powers, neither the present nor the future, neither the world above nor the world below – there is nothing in all creation that will ever be able to separate us from the love of God which is ours through Christ Jesus our Lord.' (Romans 8:38,39; *Good News Bible*)

Almost every child knows his parents will never stop loving him and they will do all they can to help him always know this. Sometimes a child has been separated from his mother, for example the premature baby who is in an incubator or is sick. Or he may have been born in circumstances where the medical staff whisked the baby away for mother to rest. The baby feels lost and loses all knowledge of security. He does not at that point know mother's love because he only experiences his own feeling: she is not there; he is lost. The emotional bonding that happens just after birth is essential to the well-being of the mother–child love relationship.

It is an old wives' tale that if you allow your child to stay with you as much as he wants he will grow dependent on you. In fact, the opposite is true. If you allow him to stay with you he will grow freely from the foundation of security and will become less dependent. If you push him away before he is ready, you will create insecurity at the very root of his being.

How does the child receive this love? I have found communication to be important, especially as it touches the senses. The smile of the parents as they catch sight of him, the words they speak as they are with him, the food he eats, and the touch he feels, all tell the child he is loved. Most important to note is touch: holding and hugging, lying close, the affectionate caress. Probably touch is not more important than the other senses, but for so long in our Western culture we have denied it. Yet the baby, whose whole body was contained and continually touched by the mother's in the womb, needs to continue to receive love through touch. Indeed, through our whole lives feeling loved is significant. Do not restrict affection and touch to marriage partners, but draw children into expressing love affectionately, with you and with others. They will learn through experiencing your friendships and the affection in them. Consider your own ability to express love, and you may well find that to the degree you are unable to express it physically you are also unable to put it into words. The two go together.

The love which the child receives establishes the foundation for growth in love relationships, which takes place parallel to other areas of growth.

TOOLS FOR FRIENDSHIP

Growing in love relationships includes the acquisition of certain skills.

There are many non-verbal expressions of friendship that develop into communication, but normally a person needs words as well, to get past misunderstandings. Non-verbal forms of communication include a look, a touch, a gift, a smile. Yet as adults, while we may realise that these are foundational forms of communication, without words we have problems. I may pass a plate to you, and between us we drop it. It is hard even to investigate how it got dropped without words. 'I thought you had it. . . .' 'I thought *you*. . . .' Through words, the situation can be unravelled. Being thinking creatures, people need words to communicate with all of themselves. Both problem solving and reflection require thinking. When we are involved in a relationship, with mutual problems and reflection, we must be able to talk to and with each other.

From the earliest moments of your child's existence, talk about yourself, your relationship to him and your relationship to others. Let him be with you when you are with other people so he will experience more words and their usage. Read or tell stories and poems and rhymes. Words are invaluable. They are the cement of friendship.

SKILLS IN RELATIONSHIPS

For the tools of relationship to be effective there must be room for skills to be acquired. First efforts with any tools are, to say the least, ham-fisted, though children are less embarrassed than adults at their first efforts. The skills of conversation and communication develop through use. So, too, does the ability to communicate the depth of friendship. When a child is with adults who are friends with each other, he will experience their communication and their affection and love for one another. He will become aware of their ways of solving problems and their ways of reflecting together. If the child is to learn from this situation, a change of approach on the part of the adult may well be necessary, for many parents consider only certain types of communication appropriate while a child is present. It is important that the child also experience other adults than his parents, perhaps friends of parents, where relationship skills are active. This is traditionally possible among relatives, aunts and uncles, in the family, but not often with the church family.

In adults' friendships with children, be the adults parents or not, there is a good arena for learning skills. The adult knows how to work things out and can draw the child into these skills, from his own knowledge. Examples are listening to each other as well as speaking, and finding solutions to problems *together*.

At Post Green camps there is an adult with each small group of children. 'Now, just a minute, let's listen to John' is one way of handling a situation. Or, 'And what other suggestions do we have? How shall we decide what to do?'

The adult may see an obvious answer, but does not bypass the opportunity for adult and child to find a mutually acceptable solution; not even with a small child.

In a child's learning of relation skills the opportunity to play with other children is vital. I have found that children who have no brothers and sisters find working together with peers very hard. Working with a small group of children, ages four to seven, I found the one 'only child' had the most difficulty in sharing. So the more opportunity to be with others the better.

At the time when children begin to play with others of the same age, they go through various stages. First a child plays individually with no reference to the other child. He may notice the other child, but the 'game' each plays bears no real relation to the other. While we may think of them as friends, one plays on the bike, while the other digs in the sand, and so on. In their imagining and their experience they are separate.

Later, as they grow, the two children want to play together. They now play in parallel. They play side by side, but careful observation reveals that they are still playing with individual projects. They talk to each other, may fight for a particular spade or brick, but build separately. They do, however, appreciate one another's company.

Later still, they begin to make one project together, be it a sandcastle or whatever. They cannot reach this stage without experiencing the others.

Some of the difficulties I observe between young children (under school age) happen when two children are 'playing together' and one has worked through the earlier stages while the other has not. The benefit of a Playgroup where there are lots of children is that each child can end up with another who is at the same stage of development.

Growth in this pattern of play is a question of opportunity and experience. I think it is a question of saying, 'Give the child the opportunity and *let him do the growing*.' I meet many parents who provide opportunities that look good, but underneath they are really trying to make their child into the most mature, the most acceptable, the most. . . . Their love is based on their own need to be superior, which results in a requirement that their child excel. I find myself hurt on behalf of the child.

CONFLICT – HOW CAN WE DEAL WITH IT?

In a previous chapter I mentioned the question of conflict. The child who has grown freely in friendships to the point of wanting to play with another child, on a joint game or project, will want to resolve conflict. How does he learn?

Firstly, have I, the helping adult, learned to deal with conflict creatively? What do I do when I disagree with someone? Do I fight to get my own way, try to insist on my way? Do I withdraw hurt when I don't win?

Secondly, is my child old enough and mature enough to sort out conflict? Do not expect your three year old to be able to settle their own differences; you will have to do this for them.

Let me illustrate. Matthew and Jenny, both three and a half, were playing in the sandpit outside the house. Both reached for the same car at the same time. Jenny's hand reached it first. Matthew looked as if he would grab it, saw Jenny's face, and burst into tears. 'Mummy, I want the red car and Jenny's got it!' Grabbing the car would have ruined the friendship feeling, but staying friendly meant not having the car. They were not old enough to work out such a conflict, so an adult said, 'Jenny, when you've had a go with the car, would you let Matthew have a go?'

Thirdly, what are the steps to sorting out disagreement and how will my child learn them?

The tension that results in conflict is normally, 'I know what I want, and I want him to do it with me, and he won't.' The individuals' 'wants' do not match, while the two persons do want to play together. The creativity or even the friendship seems to be in jeopardy.

Eventually, they will reach the maturity where they will find their own compromise solution. Matthew may say to Jenny, 'Can I have it after you?' Or an adult can help them keep talking and listening till they come up with a workable suggestion. Ask first one child, then the other, to say how he feels and what he suggests, and keep going till they are speaking to each other and not to you, and trying to find common ground.

Children can only reach a solution when they are able to realise how another person feels. You cannot make them see how another person feels, you can only wait for it to happen. All the preaching in the world will not make a child read. When he is ready he will read, and if you push too soon, any infant teacher will tell you, the result will be word-blindness. So, too, with friendship and the feelings of others: there is a time of readiness. When a child reaches this stage he will find ways to adapt his own choices. Until then, however, he will neither find it acceptable to play alone and have what he wants, nor play with another and adapt the want. He will be frustrated.

In our study of Peace, we have realised how important is our learning to solve problems together. This is now structured into much of our work with children at camps, as small groups of children plan their activities *as a group*.

Be careful that your own principles do not get in the way of the children's learning. For a younger child, you may decide that you will keep life peaceful by making a rule. With older children, you must allow them to work this out through experience, dealing with their own tension and wish to play together.

It can be quite worrying when one child is always so much in need of playing with others that he allows himself to be pushed around or victimised by them. This is not good for either op-pressor or oppressed. If the 'victim' is your own child, consider carefully what insecurity it is that makes him so desperate for friendship. Similarly, if your child is the one doing the pushing, consider what makes him feel the need to dominate. How can you help him to consider what the other child feels? Do not do this in anger or as a punishment, especially if he is not yet mature enough to sense another person's feelings. Make a rule instead; that limits the negative behaviour.

When you find a child withdrawing angrily, even silently, from conflict or tension, use a listening approach that encourages the child to tell you how he feels. He may find that the feelings can be coped with, and he will go back to the game.

Every love relationship has its painful points as it grows. So, too, with a child's friendships. It is most important that he find ways to cope with growth and his tears. Release of feelings through expressing them enables us to manage tensions and pressures.

The intervention of an adult in children's conflicts is good when the adult helps uncover the feelings. His presence can encourage (not command) listening to and understanding of one another, and then the children are free to find a creative solution.

It cannot be said too many times that for an adult to try to solve everything *for* the children denies them opportunity to grow in love.

CO-OPERATION

The ability to sort out conflict gives a child and his friends a chance to work on projects as a gang or team. Between the ages of eight and twelve a child may reach this stage if he has been given the opportunity to work through all the previous, more foundational ones. (Some children whose environment includes many and different relationships through early childhood may reach this stage earlier.)

Children will make plans to play together and say, 'What shall we do?' They know there are lots of possible, enjoyable choices. It is the *together* that is important.

Many of the co-operative tasks that our children set themselves at our camps are quite ambitious adventures, like building of tree houses, dens, models and games, or the devising of plays and other dramatic projects. Since growth is such an interweaving development, it is often possible for a group of children to have such a project set in their school or club and through it learn together to sort out conflicts. For example, through situational drama and improvisation they may as a group learn to find alternative solutions, and then to select the one they can work with.

In the informal setting of home, children, in their own play, begin to look for solutions and new ways of seeing situations. With the continuing model of the parents' relationships as a background they may look for only occasional help.

This working together is a critical stage of growth. In the child it is based on a deep, spontaneous wish to play and be with others. Yet it is also a fairly mature step on the way to adult, committed relationships. Even before teenage years, children will sometimes stick with a friendship through crisis. One child's fear or ambition will seem to produce a situation in which the other seems continually to get second best. It takes commitment to get through this. But children can. Several years ago, when she was a young teenager, my daughter said, 'Jane's in a bad mood all the time these days; I wonder what's wrong and what I can do.' The creative solutions may seem to come from only one person for a while, but friendship now is valued for itself and the tensions are less traumatic. The tensions themselves help build the value of the friendship, of give and take. This is a far step from the Matthew and Jenny situation. A four year old would say, 'Jane's horrid; I'm not going to play with her.' Growth to commitment, sticking together when it is hard, is the foundation for committed relationships such as in the church or in marriage. No person is ready for marriage before he can cope with relationship tensions in a mature way.

The support for the individual among parents and other adults at this stage is more of the reflective kind. New ways of understanding another person or situation, new ways of thinking and encouragement will result. Strong friendships with more than one person is a must, for without other friendships no one friendship is secure. Everyone, adult or child, must know to whom he can turn for help when things are difficult and with whom he can share the good things, the joys of a friendship.

While life tends to be busy, with each member of the family working out his own schedule and priorities, family time is important. This applies both to time for parent and child, and for the whole family together. While the family members, especially children, may not need constant intervention they do need to know that in the background are others who love and are actively interested in them, people who know and care where they are as well as about their sorrows and joys. This is more than discipline.

In knowing that someone, even if not present, is aware and concerned, a young adult has a continuing sense of being loved and of belonging. Growing into adulthood does not separate us from God's love. In fact, parent and child become friends, adult friends.

RESPONSIBLE LOVE

Adults in the church – and here I include those children who have reached an ability to stick together through problems – find themselves laying down their lives for their friends. Jesus, however, challenged his people to go further and love their enemies, too, which means loving those who cannot or will not love in return.

There are many who seek power, always insisting on their own way, demanding that we love them. Funnily enough we tend to *follow* the powerful, to love those who are well loved or from whom we feel love. We love the important ones since their love for us, if offered, will make us feel better about ourselves. Yet Jesus talked of others, and our enemies. To grow to consistent, sacrificial love a person must first have gone through all the other stages of receiving love and of growing. The adult who finds she wants to have a baby in order to feel loved has not got the necessary foundation of love in her own life to offer selfless love.

The mature person understands himself and is in charge of himself in his relationships. The mature person may find himself demanding or wanting a particular affirming response from a child. Recognising this, he neither blames himself nor the child. He sits down with an adult friend to consider what is going on. What inner pressure is he responding to?

The mature person understands his sexual and romantic responses. What it means to have a committed relationship is understood. So he can consider romantic relationships before being swept away by romantic feelings or strong sexual responses. He knows with which friend he can talk and be understood from a broad perspective. He knows, too, the principles that are maintained by his church, and how to work on integrating these within his own relationships.

The mature person can also take responsibility for helping someone deprived of love, whether child or adult. Through his other friendships, he will be able to recognise when he cannot help another person and is under pressure himself, just like the mother who suddenly realises that her own weariness makes her less loving towards her baby.

In all these situations adult friendship between peers is that which sustains and supports relationships, especially those that make demands. Marriage and parenthood, for example, are relationships that need the support of other friendships – deep, strong, committed friendships.

Understanding and knowing each other, however sympathetic we are towards one another, comes only with time spent together. Therefore, mature persons in friendship with one another will spend time together both in work and relaxation, and will give their friendship quite a high priority since it is supportive to their meeting the many emotional demands and needs of others.

Section Three

HEALING

Chapter 6
HOPE FOR OUR CHILDREN

> It is worth any sacrifice
> however great or costly,
> to see eyes that were listless
> light up again;
> to see someone smile
> who seemed to have forgotten
> how to smile;
> to see trust reborn
> in someone
> who no longer believed
> in anything
> or Anyone.
>
> **Dom Helder Camara**

God's work of restoration among his people has been and still is a broad and deep renewal.

God created a world into which came sin, permeating life in each of us. Because of sin, people have become trapped, and structures have resulted that hold people in separation, isolated and hurt. The work of Jesus Christ has always been to show God's purpose for people, and not just showing a picture but demonstrating by his earthly life that this life is within the reach of the church. As we work to discover wholeness as expressed in Jesus, through the work of the Spirit we are able to choose a better way than sin. Maturity means not so much that the temptation to choose sin is gone, or even that it gets less, but that the person learns to choose the way of life. Therein lies the link with responsibility. In this sense Jesus was tempted as we are, but chose not to sin.

Sin is always in us and is expressed in our choices to be greedy, or unforgiving, or violent. Sin is also in the structures around us that deny life. Defensiveness and protectiveness, which in worldly terms seem essential for survival, are destructive of positive life choices, since they keep people separated. Yet these negative aspects of society's structures also control what our children can do.

Ideally, each child should be cared for so that her wholeness will be matured. She would thus be enabled to choose life. As a parent I know my fears have in various ways denied my daughter the possibility of growth. Without meaning to, without being able to change, I have reproduced and fed the sinful nature; so has every other parent. Being imperfect ourselves we can do no other. We are imperfect parents of imperfect children. So in my child, in our children, there is both life and death at work, just as in the parable of the wheat and tares. These will not be finally separated or cleared up till we reach heaven. If we destroyed the part that allows for sinful choices, the child herself would be destroyed.

So what are we to do?

Very much like St. Paul we find ourselves torn. The good we would like to do we find we cannot do. Fortunately, God has set us free from the slavery to death. Within us as God's people is the Spirit who will give us life (Romans 8). We, who recognise the sin in us, may believe the redemptive grace of God. The Spirit has shown us that deep in us can be life from God, that knowledge of belonging to him, which urges us to call God 'Abba, Father'. We can become God's children. In Jesus, we his people, are redeemed. Not just today, but past, present and future. Sin no longer holds us bound, on the path to death.

GOD AT WORK

The redeeming work of Christ is renewing us in many ways, at many levels, and our children, too.

One evening I found myself sitting next to a friend, who was both pregnant and ill and was in a wheelchair. I found myself telling her of my experience with a little girl called Susann. Susann was a baby who, when just a few weeks old, was temporarily separated from her mother. Part of my work became to look after her. I sensed but did not really know how much this separation could affect Susann. So I decided that I must love her with all the love her own mother would give her. She was constantly in my awareness and care. One particular feature of my job at that time involved answering the phone for the Community where

I lived. I was the 'receptionist'. We lived in a large and rambling old house; calls came for people who, because of their work, were scattered all over the house and grounds. Thus, each day, whether she was waking or sleeping, I often picked up Susann and took her with me, for I would not leave her on her own. I carried her up and down stairs or to the garden or wherever I could expect to find the recipient of the phone call.

I told my friend that I believed my response to the original 'instinct' to keep Susann close had prevented her from suffering the kind of deep insecurity that can result from even a temporary 'loss' of mother at that age.

My friend's eyes filled with tears. 'I can hardly believe it,' she said. 'The circumstances around my birth were such that I felt totally separated from my mother and her love. When God wanted to heal me of that pain, which I've always had, he showed me himself carrying me around, never putting me down and leaving me. He didn't just feed me and then leave; he took me with him. That's what happened for Susann with you. He spoke to you and your carrying her around was God's redemption for her, when otherwise she would have felt just as hurt as I have so often.'

God had been at work when otherwise the situation would have hurt Susann very deeply. The sharing of the story made both my friend and me more aware of God's redemptive work in us and our children.

GUILT

In the last few years I have discovered many many things I could have felt guilty about, things I've failed to do in bringing up my child. Yet God has shown me how he is working in her, often as he is working in me, integrating, redeeming and healing. He has offered life to her in a fuller and fuller way as I have been changed, healed and renewed. I see this as a constant process, so I do not think I should feel guilty. Rather I recognise my own growing ability to choose life when faced with a choice. Whatever patterns of death my daughter lives out through her attitudes and actions God's grace has redeemed and is renewing. And the integration of what God is saying to me in my life has subsequently helped her.

Over these last few years I have also found that my Christian family have supported and sustained this growth pattern.

GROWTH TO OUR FULL POTENTIAL

God is at work to change and redeem. In each of us there are aspects of life where we have not grown. What was necessary for growth was never provided. Unknowingly or fearfully parents withheld or did not know how to provide what was needed for growth.

Let us consider the need for growth, firstly by looking at the result of its not being met. *Love and security* are at the root of feeling good about oneself and life. To be deprived of such love results in the child losing her sense of being, of identity, of belonging. This may result, for instance, when mother or baby, before or after birth, is ill, *or when* they are separated immediately after birth so that bonding does not take place. Or it may happen that the mother finds herself feeling unable to love her baby. So baby loses that sense of being loved that is God's purpose for her.

New experience comes as a result of opportunity to go out into the exciting world around. There is baby's curiosity, there is challenge and adventure. If this new experience is absent, the child is understimulated and growth is limited. For example, a child who is given no opportunity to play with children of her own age, will continually find relationships difficult. The child who has no books around her, no stories, will have difficulty learning to read at school. So too with colour, music and all kinds of play opportunities. So too with getting out into the neighbourhood and shops, on bus outings and so on. If never introduced to these the child will grow with a limited and diminished potential.

Praise and recognition. A child should be recognised and valued for who she is and what she can do. Praise and encouragement will feed the natural force for growth in her, enabling her to find her full potential. Competition will destroy this. Each child in a competitive situation is compared to others and valued according to what 'similar' children are doing or achieving. 'Johnny has three teeth; that's better than Martin, he has not got any teeth yet!' 'Jane can already write her own name, before starting school, and Susan can't, and she has been at school for three months.' Such value systems are very destructive. The winners today, Johnny and Jane, sense that they will be less acceptable if they do not win. Conversely, the losers feel smaller and less and less like the persons whom God values just as they are. The details of differing patterns and paces of growth mean that every child will do things in her own time. The inner growth mechanism, given by God, determines this.

It is not that we can never compare children in an objective way. For example, what do I expect many five year olds to be doing? There is going to school, learning to read and write, drawing, painting, cutting and sticking and lots of other activities. I then provide many opportunities for these for each child. *But* I must not value the children according to which they tackle first or most. If a child seems slow, for example, in reading, I must find a way to help her, not because this makes her a failure or a fool, but because I think this person would enjoy the stories she could then read.

So competition, its values and attitudes, destroys a person's sense of self-worth and produces a sense of failure and self-rejection.

Responsibility is a key to choosing life and is given to each child as she grows. Step by step and stage by stage she acquires the tools and experience necessary for being a responsible member of church and society. This is not an overnight event but a process of gradual and continuous growth. It is very easy for parents to continue to make decisions for their children, which the children could well make for themselves. The result of continuing to do this will be that the child will lack determination, since she will not have had the opportunity to follow through on her own decisions. She will always doubt herself. A friend of mine, when thinking of this, said she wished she had had a chance to make her first decisions when she was young, then she could have learned how. Instead, when she got to eighteen and began making decisions, they were in areas of life important enough for the results to be disastrous. So many adults are afraid of making decisions, especially when those decisions will affect the lives of other people.

Healthy growth in decision-making is an on-going process throughout childhood, as the child accepts more and more responsibility.

TRAUMATIC EXPERIENCES

Every child can potentially have had her growth needs met,

75

and still run into an experience that disturbs her deeply, so deeply that her subsequent approach to life is distorted, even subconsciously. It may be an illness, the death of someone close, or an accident. Something has caused the child to show symptoms of deep unrest and inability to cope.

Within any book it is impossible to cover the whole field of understanding what healing can mean among children. Here I am only going to give a few pointers and recommend some possible courses of action.

Any child may show occasional signs of disturbance and distress for short periods, signs such as continued anger, frustration, bed-wetting, consistent disobedience, school problems, listlessness, friendship problems, shyness, depression. These are not all indications that the child has gone 'off the rails', and needs major intervention to sort things out.

One of the key jobs of childhood, and even adulthood, is 'coping'. (I have found Dr. Frank Lake especially helpful on this subject.) This involves the person finding her own creative means for dealing with problems and difficulties. When a problem crops up the person may register her own negative reactions, through the signs listed above. But soon, and perhaps with a little help, she will overcome or find a creative way of *coping* with the circumstances and feelings. When this particular learning is happening the other person should not interfere, though he or she can keep a watchful eye on her, ready to encourage.

Sometimes parents worry about things that are really very normal in children, things they would not worry about at all if they only knew this. But what if the symptoms are persistent and there really is something wrong?

Listening and observing are important. What is my child saying through her actions as well as her words? I can try to listen from a fresh starting point. Maybe I should consider the growth opportunities I am making available. Broadly taking the many aspects of her life into consideration, is it time to offer more?

Is this child expressing her reactions to basic disagreements between her parents and their problems? Does she get one message from Mum and a different one from Dad? Or are there hostilities in their relationship that are being 'hidden' from the child which they are unable to sort out?

Let me think back over the previous weeks and months, during or before my child's signs of distress. Were there events in our family life that she might still feel hurt about, for example moving house, starting school, a death, a divorce or another event, that could have resulted in strong feelings? The strong feelings, if not coped with, will cause such symptoms.

Let me consider whether there are attitudes I maintain that could be making her feel unacceptable to me. Did I want a boy, not a girl? Do I want her to excel at school? Or to be friendly and outgoing? Do I want her to be my kind of person?

Let me pray, asking God to show me what might be the cause of the child's pain and distress. Read well-informed books about children. Here again friends are important. Knowing both me as parent and my child, they may have helpful ideas. I listen carefully to schoolteachers, playgroup leaders, health visitors or others who work with children.

Receiving the child. I keep two quotes on the wall above my desk, both from A. S. Neill's *Summerhill*. The first one reads, 'Curing a neurosis in a child is a matter of the release of the emotion, and the cure will not be furthered in any way by expounding ... theories to the child and telling him he has a complex.' The other says, 'At Summerhill, it is love that cures: it is approval and the freedom to be true to oneself.'

An example: When a child feels grief it is best for her to express it, with all she is. Comfort must never try to stop the feeling, or try to make her feel better. Be there as a friend till the child has finished grieving. Similarly, if a child is angry she must express her feeling, with all the hurt and pain she feels. I never let any child hurt me or others as she expresses this, but I must accept her *with her feeling*. So if she hurls herself crying onto her bed, I stay with her but do not stop her crying.

Many of the traumas that happen do result in too many reactions, or too big a reaction, for the child to cope. The way she responds to them is to repress the feelings, packing them away subconsciously. Unfortunately, they later creep out in life patterns, or in the distress symptoms above.

When a child shows consistent signs of disturbance and simple changes in family attitude seem insufficient, it may well be time to seek professional help. This may seem embarrassing, but this may be the way that God's healing power will be available to the child. The kind of therapy offered through professional channels is normally excellent. Contact your family doctor for reference to an appropriate specialist or contact the head teacher of your child's school. There are many ways your child can be helped to release feelings and cope. Some organisations will work with the whole family, as the family structures may be causing the difficulty.

PARENTS CAN HELP

As I have discovered weaknesses in my child that continue to trap her, like self-rejection or fears, I have realised I must take a close look at myself. Is her weakness a repetition of a weakness that is in me? In helping me with my own weakness, God has helped her. Thus I have pursued my own renewal and growth, and this has created a more effective environment for her. For example, we must recognise the depth of our own guilty feelings about our children. In whatever way is appropriate we must confess and repent and find absolution. This will open a space where something new can happen. If we condemn ourselves so much that we can do nothing, we, and our child, will continue to feel hurt.

Find someone who can help you in this, whether a minister or a mature Christian friend. Whichever is your way, receive God's healing grace, for he shares in the pain you and your child live with.

Prayer, as a communion and reflection with God, is healing and renewing. I have found a retreat or quiet day a good time to sit with God and tell him all about me, my hopes and expectations, my failures and guilt, my longing and my wish for his help.

Pray for your child. Sit on her bed when she is asleep. Gently speak to her of the things you have talked to God about, how you feel he is giving you both new life, pray for healing of your hurts.

Again because of the depth of our feelings for our children it is helpful to have a friend, a 'soul friend', who will pray with us with our child, helping us keep faith and perspective.

Our own walk with God, our life of prayer, will actually be the most helpful aspect of developing a place of healing and growth for children. As our life with Christ is rooted in our everyday experience, so our children will receive life.

HANDICAPPED AND SICK CHILDREN

Prayer for physical healing is just as relevant for children as for adults. But what of those who are not healed? Our response is often hurt, embarrassment and disillusionment. Also, we are conditioned by a powerful cultural pressure that demands and affirms physical perfection.

I would like to quote from John H. Westerhoff III in *Bringing Up Children in the Christian Faith*:

The norm for human life should not be the physically attractive and capable adult, not the mentally bright, rational adult, not the emotionally stable adult. We would understand human life better if the norm were the exceptional physically, emotionally, mentally retarded child. When we begin our understanding of human life with the fully functioning adult we strive to manipulate the 'normal' child to be like us, and we depreciate and patronize the 'abnormal' child because he or she can never be like us. We need to affirm that we are all exceptional children and that they represent what it means to be human. In that important sense true maturity is being what we are to the fullest. If we have been blessed with physical, emotional, mental, or behavioural gifts, then more will be expected of us, but we will not be of any greater value. Indeed, only as we remember, recapture, and live out the exceptional child in ourselves will we be fully human.

Each child, whatever her physical or emotional state, is fully a person. Each can live fully and joyfully within the limits of her abilities. It is for adults to discover and offer her opportunity. We may recognise that God does not wish this child to suffer, nor did he wish sin in the world to have this effect, but it has and it will. It is up to us to challenge the power of sin, in our attitudes to those who are handicapped, and also in looking for healing through medical, social and educational ways, as well as through miraculous ways.

If you have a handicapped child in your family or church, work out how to give her the fullest opportunity for growth, as the person she is. As a family and church, begin to talk to God about the child and let him lead and speak to you. You will find yourselves at a new place of acceptance and love that will bring joy to many children.

Section Four

A SENSE OF GOD

Chapter 7
SPIRITUAL FOUNDATIONS

Happy Thought

The world is so full
of a number of things,
I'm sure we should all
be as happy as kings.

Robert Louis Stevenson

Over the last few years as I have reflected on my early life, I have remembered times of confusion and isolation. My cry to God has been, 'Why were you not there when I needed you? And you say you care about children!' I heard him say, 'I was there, but no one showed you where I was.' This was an absolute revelation to me of God's presence continually, his word reaching out, the Spirit hovering close. Now, the focus for me is not on whether God is present and speaks, but whether I am listening or able to listen.

With children around me, am I helping them to enjoy knowing themselves in God's family, becoming aware of God's presence?

For each child to have a sense of who God is requires no change in God; he is present with the child, he does not have to start being present. Rather, there falls on us adults a responsibility to introduce them to one another.

This chapter, then, is about introductions and foundations to a child's growing sense of God's presence, and what will help a child in this.

We shall primarily consider the foundations in the child, touching on many aspects of the parents' quality of life. For this, in reality, will determine the quality of life for the dependent child.

The notion of relationship to God being experiential as well as intellectual, subjective as well as objective, feeling as well as thought, is not new to Christianity. That children can or should receive the elements at Eucharist, or belong to the church is not new either. I thought that both concepts might be totally new until I began to discover the breadth of the history of God's people and the breadth of present-day expression of his life. Some of these principles with which we grapple so determinedly are central premises of other branches of the church.

The child is primarily dependent on his parents, and through the parents on the church. His faith, his life in God, will not grow fully without the work and structures and supportive environment of the church. What does the church environment offer to the family and the child along with the belonging and the full involvement in corporate worship of the church? These are indeed critical, for they affirm God's attitude and interest in the child, but the other complementary and vital aspect is the child's response to God. To care for this is the pastoral work of the church.

Often where children are concerned such care is given by the parents. The church, however, has pastoral responsibility for the whole family, and the family is responsible to it. Children are the weak, dependent members who need nuclear and church families to be working together in a well-functioning relationship. This is the context in which the response of the child to God is based.

Karl Rahner, in *Theological Investigations*, vol. 8, 1971, sees childhood as a phase in the life of a person. Every person is growing and learning and experiencing God's life. Each stage has its own value; it is not valuable only as a step to another. Many aspects of a responsible, mature development of relationship to God are not developed in the child. They will only happen as the child eventually comes to take full responsibility for himself as an adult. The following quote speaks of the individual growing in knowledge of his own identity organically and individually.

To be a parent is to be open and giving. It is to nurture, not to process or indoctrinate. Then the child will no longer need a parent. Kahlil Gibran, in *The Prophet*, says,

> You may give your love but not your thoughts
> For they have their own thoughts.
> You may house their bodies but not their souls
> For their souls dwell in the house of tomorrow,
> Which you cannot visit, nor even in your dreams.
> You may strive to be like them, but seek not to make
>   them like you.

For life goes not backward nor tarries with yesterday.
You are the bows from which your children as living
  arrows are sent forth.

FOUNDATIONS

Through the loving commitment of parents and other church
members and involvement with other children, the child learns to
live in relationships. He learns to make choices that may limit
him but further his friendships. He learns to resolve differences
and to give love when none is returned. The same kinds of skills
will help his relationship to God.

Through the continuing experience of life each person
receives a picture of his own gifts and abilities. He finds creativity
in himself. Through daily interaction in experience with people,
with reality, with decision-making and challenge the child gains a
picture of himself.

The self-discipline of living close to God cannot be separated
from relationships with others. The childhood experience of recognising the identity, validity and value of another person helps
the small child know that he himself is not God, and that he is on
the path to discovery of the meaning of his own life.

What is the purpose of life? Who is the person who established its order, its patterns, its strengths and weaknesses? God is
the focus of all life, and each person, on realising this, chooses
to live in harmony with God, or to live in alienation from God.
It takes a lifetime of discovery to know something of who God
is.

What is the meaning of life for parents? Is his or her purpose
to live in harmony with God? If the parents' purpose does not lie
in growing in their own relationship to God, the child will not be
helped.

Let us consider parents for a moment. Many women I meet
have not seen themselves as persons in their own right, as children
of God. They live as if it were only when they perform certain
roles, like those of wife and mother, that they have a significant
purpose for their lives or value in themselves. Yet God all the
while loves us for who we are. Being on the receiving end in this
kind of situation, the child feels very significant. 'I am so important that my mother rushes to meet my every need, to do all I
want. So everyone should do everything I want.' The woman

who finds her meaning in God, however, functions fully in the roles of wife and mother, but the child is aware of a deeper reality in the purpose of life. Mother's life centres on God, not on the child. To centre it on the child makes the child a god. Similarly, if the father focuses his life and meaning on God, he can begin to release the child into being the way God created him to be.

The child, in experiencing these persons whose identity is in God, will grow, and will later find it easier to consider his own friendship with God.

PATTERNS AND RHYTHMS

The patterns of childhood can give support to a peaceful life with God. Kenneth Leech talks of the 'rhythms of life' in adults. Patterns and rhythms of everyday life are either easy or difficult, depending on childhood experiences. The patterns of eating and sleeping and of time-keeping are examples.

Eating is a primary need to which many emotions are attached. I have noticed that family mealtimes are sometimes friendly and easy-going times, when we can hear from each other and inquire of each other. The food is offered with love by the one who cooked, with the interests and tastes of the family in mind, a variety and a homeliness that encourages and affirms each member, including the cook. On the other hand there are times when there is argument, a battle of wills over whether the child will or will not eat this or that. Many barriers to peace can grow around food.

If food is used as a means of emotional bribery or compensation (chocolates and sweets often are), many disturbing emotions grow. 'Do eat this up. I've made a special dessert for you, but you cannot have any unless you eat this! It is good for you. . . .' So what's 'good' for the child seems opposite and compensated for by what is sweet and enjoyable. The various polarisations of feelings expressed in this situation will later affect the adult relationship to God: 'If I do what God wants me to do, this good, obedient act, I'll deserve and be owed a reward, a nice dessert.' That is a lie. We deserve nothing, as Jesus says in the parable. Similarly, many parents who compensate for their own sense of guilt or lack of love by giving sweets and chocolate build another destructive attitude: 'I must have. . . .' A near 'addiction' in some adults is really an expression of feeling unloved, a situation that needs resolution before life in relation to God can grow.

Sleep is the peaceful resting of the person at the end of the day, a day fulfilled. To sleep in peace renews the person, prepares him for the new day ahead. The psalmist says that 'God gives to his beloved sleep'. For a child to sleep peacefully, bedtime itself should be a peaceful reflection on the day, a time of communion. When Jacqueline was small we often talked over the day together after tea or at storytime as she went to bed. On the days I was distracted by my own thoughts or was anxiously hurrying her off, this time was peaceful for neither of us. It was really much better on those days that we laughed and remembered together, till we said a prayer together and I went downstairs.

A peaceful bedtime is the assurance to the child that sleep and its inherent separation from consciousness is not a breaking of love. The onset of sleep and darkness does not mean separation from the parents' love. This in itself helps allay fears of darkness. The child will have dreams, even nightmares, but the knowledge that a parent is within call, a parent who loves him and can re-introduce reality to the dream world, takes the edge off the fear. In the adult, subsequently, 'the dark night of the soul' is not so much a place of fears but a place in which to expect the one who loves. The vision or horrors that may invade the mind of an adult will not have the same power if the child's sleeping is such a time of communion.

It follows that bedtime should not be a punishment. The child should not be sent to bed in disgrace. The resolution of the break in communion between parent and child must happen before bedtime. Then sleep can become a quieting and peaceful end to a day and the refreshing beginning to the next.

The pattern of the day, the pattern of life is a movement that can flow gently and freely. Is there a peaceful rather than abrupt beginning to the day, with maybe a busy (but not frantic) break-fast time, a settled though maybe excited setting-out from home, a homecoming when each feels received as a person? Is there time to play, time to eat, time to sleep without a fight against the structure? Or does the time structure, the schedule of the day, not support the individual? Does your child feel pushed, hurried through breakfast because there is too much to do before leaving, in the way at homecoming, hurried off to bed because parents have other, more important things to do? A settled and supportive schedule that has time for the person builds security of identity.

The person for whom there has never been time is continually anxious about time-tables, whether there is 'enough time for *me*'; and peace and a sense of time with God will always be pushed away by anxious thoughts.

As a parent, consider how the structures of your day meet yours and your child's needs as persons. Is there a sense of shape and rhythm, into which each of you can settle without feeling constantly pressured by factors outside your control?

REFLECTION

Reflection, which is so significant to many aspects of personal growth, easily goes by the board. After busy times, when a child gets in from school or at the end of the day, there should be time for telling all that has happened, the excitement, the joys, disappointments, adventures and hopes for tomorrow. The busyness settles in a quieter reflection and appreciation of one another and of God and life. It may even become silence together. A real rest is present in the child, physical as well as mental. It can be encouraged by quietness and gentle touch, the parent stroking the child's head. Some children like to have their backs scratched; turn this into a gentle touch so that it helps settle any inner unrest.

Such an approach to reflection and quietness together is vulnerable to outside pressures, the main cry of which is, 'It's time; come on, we must go now!' The structure of time, the schedule, should serve you, not the other way round. Obviously the family's life is lived within the wider structure of life, but negotiate both ways. If you know you are going out, be prepared to start children's bedtime and bathing a little earlier rather than cramp your child's call on your attention. Be prepared to be a little late sometimes.

Watch out if you and others are constantly irritated by your continual lateness or obsessive time-keeping. Time is running you; your life does not have a settled rhythm in which you are at home. Be at peace with time.

Recently I found myself remembering a time when waiting at Birmingham Station, when Jacqueline was not quite five. Having just missed a connection, we had two hours to wait. With no money at all we were limited to staying right where we were. I wondered, in thinking back, why she was not endlessly up and down, fussing for this and that. I found myself asking God. He showed me how much of Jacqueline's life is similar to my own. For me, that wait on the platform was interesting, peaceful, quiet and unpressured. So she was the same. We talked a little, but both were happy to watch the comings and goings of other travellers. Had I been anxious she would have been unsettled. Over the years I have seen how many times the quality of my approach to life, whether positive or negative, has been repeated in her.

ACTIVITY

Hobbies, crafts and similar activities that express a person's creativity in an unhurried and fulfilling way help growth. When I find I am constantly so busy that I have no time for these I arrive at my time of quiet with God somehow resentful about the way life is. Or I am frustrated and unable to settle my mind which skips everywhere. When I have had time to relax, whether knitting or gardening, I feel quite different. Within a family, when there is a chance, relax together, walk or talk, play and read stories. Encourage handcrafts that challenge the individual while expressing creativity.

The foregoing presents a picture of a very settled and relaxed family life. But it may not be quite so straightforward.

DISCIPLINE

Within everyone in the family there are threads that reflect the sin within us. Not just our limitations as parents, but our sin and our child's sin. Each adult is responsible for his own sin, to see sin and its effects and for finding the redeeming grace at work in his or her life.

Additionally, I am responsible for sin with respect to my child. I am responsible for seeing that sin, in her, in the family and in the world, does not climb up like a weed and choke life out of her. As I look for God's grace to redeem my sin, so, in my relationship to her, I always try to make grace and not sin my starting point. Sometimes I see my child deliberately choose to do something bad, and I am then responsible for limiting this, as when she is plainly greedy, or determined to get better than others.

Many expressions of sin have to do with relationships and with recognising and valuing other persons. In adult terms we may talk of greed, hostility and anger, unforgiveness, etc. A constructive way of looking at these is for the adults to recognise what positive quality they wish to have for their family life and relationships, qualities such as consideration, listening, generosity and so on. My own summary of what I have worked with has been, 'We will not violate one another.' So greedy grabbing is stopped, so is endless demand for the child's own way. Physical or verbal violence is not acceptable, and this includes refusal to listen to others. But also I try hard to make sure I am not punishing immaturity.

I grew up believing in spanking when children deliberately violate the set standards, or are directly disobedient when obedience is necessary. Personally, I am now more interested in the 'time out' approach, though every family must decide for itself how it will insist on standards being kept. When family life is loving and encouraging, and attractive to the child, misbehaviour can be limited by temporary exclusion. 'Michael, I do expect you to listen. Please go into the other room until you are prepared to listen sometimes, as the rest of us do.' – 'John, please sit over here out of the game until you want to play without hitting the other children. None of us is allowed to hurt others.' I have found this a principle that works well, 'I have told you that you must ride your bike this way on the road. Until you are going to do it the way I require, I am taking away your bike. . . .'

Such an approach restricts the child at the point where he is able to live caringly and lovingly with others, yet deliberately chooses not to, and chooses to violate friendship. Using 'time out' to help a child to see and be responsible for his own deliberate choices lays the foundation for his being able to work out his life with God.

Many adults who have never considered or really dealt responsibly with their own choices cannot grasp how to deal with it in relation to God. Spiritual growth in adults then has to include much that could have been creatively experienced in childhood.

If all the requirements of a parent are seen as laws and to break them results in physical punishment, what picture will the child form of authority or of God? God will be seen as an authoritarian, who sets arbitrary laws, and when one trespasses against them there is *dire* punishment. The whole concept of a

relationship and a loving family is liable to be lost. Family discipline must include space for repentance and forgiveness. In the
Old Testament God repeatedly forgave his 'child' Israel, and only
when his people set not just individual actions but the whole
basis of their life against him did God drastically punish them, in
the Exile.

To establish a discipline, which does include obedience, and
at the same time emphasises that sin separates us from each other,
is to make a creative foundation for life. For life in relationship
to God, that is. Jesus' commandment to love God and love your
neighbour summarises the whole Law. The simple reason for these
rules of love is that sin breaks relationship. Discipline that grows
to self-discipline in relationships will emphasise the positive
aspects of maintaining love, not simply outward conformity. The
'time out' principle helps this very effectively.

INHERITANCE

Sometimes I have found that my child's inconsistency or
misdemeanours are very related to mine! When I do not listen to
others, she won't. When I am requiring of her what I do not do
myself we always run into difficulties. Where I find a consistent
problem I ask myself several questions: Am I expecting too much,
more than this child can yet do? What should I do to help her?
Or should I let it drop till she is older and more mature?

Then I ask myself, 'Am I asking this child to do what I do
not do, or what we adults do not do?' The Open University course
The Pre-School Child offers a good example. Do you require
your child to share his toys with a visitor and find he will not do
it? Do you share your tools, your make-up, your chocolate, or
does the child experience you in a subtle way keeping your be-
longings from others? When a visitor is coming, could you put
out something of yours for him to play with, thus offering a
positive example? If I give an invitation and expect this to mean
sharing, it will happen only if my child experiences me doing it
first. Then he will grow to doing it freely himself. I would not, do
not, allow a child to invite a playmate and then not allow the
visitor to play with the toys. To invite means to include.

As two parents, consider the following, as an example: Let
us say that you, Mum, get cross that your child has come in yet
again with dirty wellingtons. Is Dad expecting a different standard

by coming in in his dirty wellingtons? Two standards in one family are not helpful.

FORGIVENESS

Probably the most all-encompassing aspect of relationship to God that has its foundation in childhood is forgiveness. Jesus expressed God's forgiveness to the world in his own life and death. In relationship to his disciples he both taught and forgave. Growth and learning through experience include many mistakes, intentional and unintentional. When they are forgiven and reflected on constructively, growth happens. Whether mistakes happen with things or in relationships, indecisions or judgments, forgiveness is the quality that smoothes the way for positive forward movement.

In the family setting, forgiveness will first be seen in the parents relationship to each other, to their children and to others. When misunderstandings happen between Mum and Dad, such as when one does or says something the other is surprised by or disagrees with, what happens next? Is there a stony silence, an angry reaction or does one parent simply override the other? It is more helpful in such minor upsets if the children experience their parents reflecting together on what is going on and forgiving one another.

Does parents' conversation about other people contain forgiveness of their faults? When I talk about others in the church or about neighbours, as I see their faults and weakness, what do I do? Do I forgive them and still hold them high in my estimation, or do I 'cut them down to size'? Do other people's weaknesses or mistakes, bad attitudes and so on affect my friendship with them? What about children? When a child has done something wrong or made a mistake, is forgiveness my first thought? Can I first forgive them, then reflect, 'How can we learn from this?' or 'How can my child learn from this mistake?'

Forgiveness is not the same as ignoring faults, nor is it the same as punishment. Creative forgiveness involves reflection that looks for a new course of action, a new attitude or a new conclusion. When I was teaching in school, a child who did a sum wrong could be punished. But then he would have learned nothing about sums for the future. Forgiveness that ignores and would forget the mistake brings no learning. Alternatively, I could forgive the error, saying, 'This is wrong, but how can I help you work it out so you can do these sums in the future?' This kind of forgiveness is necessary for a growth situation.

God's forgiveness in Christ was the door to life. It was neither punishment nor a continuation of sin and its effects. It is the forgiveness that tackles these attitudes and actions that provide a place of growth.

Spiritual depth in adult life can, as we have seen, be founded on family attitudes and lifestyle in childhood. At the heart is forgiveness, a workable pace of life, peaceful relationships, creative activity. The fruit of these in terms of spirituality may not be seen before the child has grown to adulthood and determines his own relationship to God. Then such childhood experience can help growth.

Chapter 8
AMONG GOD'S PEOPLE

Today I saw a dandelion.
It smiled at me and said,
'God loves you, do you know?

Maggie Durran

Everyone who ever tackles the subject of a child's relationship to God will, like me, hesitate at first. Jesus' words are heavy on my mind. They are worthy of careful attention.

. . . The disciples came to Jesus, asking, 'Who is the greatest in the Kingdom of heaven?' So Jesus called a child, made him stand in front of them, and said, 'I assure you that unless you change and become like children, you will never enter the Kingdom of heaven. The greatest in the Kingdom of heaven is the one who humbles himself and becomes like this child. And whoever welcomes in my name one such child as this, welcomes me.
'If anyone should cause one of these little ones to lose his faith in me, it would be better for that person to have a huge millstone tied around his neck and be drowned in the deep sea. How terrible for the world that there are things that make people lose their faith. Such things will always happen – but how terrible for the one who causes them!' (Matthew 18:1–7; *Good News Bible*)

Other interesting references to children among Jesus' words are in Matthew 19:13–15, Mark 10:13–16 and Luke 9:46–48. Jesus shows us the child has a place in the kingdom of heaven. She belongs and is at home there. When we receive this child we receive Jesus. The child is dependent on us; it would be easy for us to cause her to stumble, or to discount her faith. Can we, the people of God, receive and nurture his child enabling her to grow fully and eventually develop her own relationship with God? At any age or stage of development there can be communion between the person and God, and expression of the trusting faith of which Jesus spoke. The nature of this expression we adults cannot easily describe, but it does exist.

RELATIONSHIPS

Jesus' words, 'faith in me', describe an active relationship. I suppose I could say I am 'related' to Margaret Thatcher. There are certain similarities: human, female, white, British, adult . . . and maybe a few more, such as a similar Christian name. But these are similarities that are not descriptive of an active relationship; that essential element of familiarity is missing.

What is this essential element of similarity in terms of our relationship to God, which should make it perfectly clear that when we receive this child we receive Jesus, not just that a series of abstract truths apply? When he talked of himself he was not seeing himself separate from the warm-blooded emotional person that he was, though he was God, too.

Faith in Jesus is a relationship to be experienced. Marriage is an experiential relationship about which we can state certain observable facts which are accepted because of experience. However, without the real experience of the consummation of the relationship the marriage may be annulled, or written off as not valid. So, too, a relationship with Jesus should be experienced in reality. Jesus states this directly in Matthew 7:21–23 and again in Matthew 25:31–46. Knowing, an active kind of knowing, is essential to a relationship of faith.

We can accumulate much information about God, but that is different from and complementary to knowing him in our experience. Just as in our human relationships our knowledge and understanding of one another is a joining of experience and information, so too with God. Theology is objective or observable facts about God, with whom a relationship is a continuing experience.

It is predictable, therefore, that the nurture of faith in a child has similarities to the nurture of other love relationships.

GOD IN US AND AROUND US

Love grows from love given to and received by the child.

Creativity grows as that aspect is considered and nurtured in the child. She is given what is necessary for growth. Responsibility and freedom are given steadily and consistently and so the child grows. So also with the child's faith, the essential part is the relationship to God. As we consistently and considerately give God's life to our children in experience, their sense of receiving God's love and grace will grow. If the essence of that love and grace is offered to the person, she can grow fully as a person, including spiritually, until eventually she can become responsible for receiving grace for her own redemption.

The context for the child is the family and the context for the family is the church. The child depends on her family, within the church family, to continually give her the food of life necessary for her growth.

WORSHIP WITH CHILDREN

Worship is the offering of ourselves to God, in everything we do, say or think. When we worship together it is a celebration of our relationship to him, our everyday life with him. We give praise and thanksgiving to him together. We hear him speak to us also, about his plans for us his family, about his advice, his caution.

The people of Israel experienced daily life with God through his everyday involvement with them. As God spoke to them in their experiences they understood his identity and relationship to them. Their children, living and experiencing this, also grew up with a sense of God's identity and presence. In the same way, our corporate worship life, our family gathering with God, opens life with God in a broad way to children. It is not that adults are simply talking about God; they are sharing their life with God so openly that the children can experience it, too.

The church family will in every way possible help the child experience God at a practical level, allowing understanding to happen as appropriate. To lead a child into involvement in the church's worship is to enable her to be part of the church's response to God and to begin to enable the child to see what her own response might be. So worship together is an opportunity to express the growing relationship between God and his family, as the context for that relationship.

What, then, are the parts of our church life and worship that nurture the life of Christ in our children? Which elements of our life can be received as they are and which ones must first be put into a form that a child can receive? Does a child have to conform to any particular form or levels of understanding in order to be able to experience the life of Christ among us?

The offering of God's love for the child also begins while the child is still unborn. Giving the mother-to-be a supportive, caring environment in turn supports the child, giving her a sense of being loved. Help may be at a practical level, such as encouragement and assistance with getting hospital appointments, caring for other children in the family. Friendship at a deep level is very important, for this enables the mother, at a time of considerable emotional vulnerability, not to store up her fears and anxieties about the expected baby or about other members of the family. In God's people gathering to worship, the unborn child receives life as her mother receives life, is part of her response to God, receives through the presence of the Spirit, through the atmosphere of the gathering and through the mother's receiving grace and life in the bread and wine of Eucharist.

BABIES IN CHURCH

From the earliest days a baby can be welcomed among the congregation at times of worship in the church. There is an official kind of welcoming in the Baptism or Dedication service. She is acknowledged and welcomed as one whom the whole church accepts as a member, belonging to them, named by them and dependent on them. There is ongoing interest in the baby, too, when this happens at the heart of the church's life.

Hannah, one of the children in Post Green Community, was baptised during our church's main service, the Sunday morning Eucharist. Her parents are regularly in the congregation so Hannah's birth was celebrated by the parish family among whom she is growing. Many people who normally have no contact with children still keep in contact with Hannah, as belonging to them.

There are other, more mundane ways to welcome the baby, too. Members of the congregation other than the parents can hold and comfort a fretful baby, or walk around outside with her if necessary. In that way parents can sometimes have a little uninterrupted time during worship, and the baby still feels quite secure. The baby can receive unconditional love from her whole family, the church, who can care, love, nurture and support in every way.

COMMUNICATION WITH GOD

First let us be aware that God is to be experienced through a variety of ways in which life is manifest. There is an individual perception of this, which is tempered by the corporate. The individual's experience or awareness of God is saved from potential fantasy by the fellowship with and submission to the whole church. So the bible, church history and present day church experiences all keep the individual relating to the real expression of God, not to a personal fantasy or dreams. The same is true of the child. The child who has not grown to the stage of separating fantasy from reality is totally dependent on the church family to know and recognise this, not as a means of 'correction', but of giving her a context that does not require a separation of these before she is included in the worship. In other words, they take responsibility for the child's perceptions and observations, receiving them with the kind of understanding with which the parent receives information about the tiger in the garden, or the imaginary playmate, yet knowing that sometimes they are of importance to everyone.

Nanette, a young single woman, and Michal Ann, aged six, both members of the same household, were chatting together. In the course of the conversation Michal Ann said something like, 'This is what the Lord says: "In the winter the trees are bare, but spring will come and there will be leaves and flowers."' Knowing both individual and corporate circumstances within the Community, Nanette recognised that Michal Ann had received a word of encouragement for everyone. She asked Michal Ann if she could draw a picture about what she had said. As a result, the Community's teaching that evening was illustrated by Michal Ann's words and drawing. More importantly, her individual life was made relevant to the whole family through the incorporation of her thoughts and ideas.

The individual relationship with God and perception of him is facilitated by shared reflection. Children's bedtime prayer has often been a kind of formal shopping list for God. This can be changed to a friendly reflection on the day in God's presence. What has God done and said in the child's experience? Adult and child can then pray together about these things.

It is helpful if the church family's corporate worship includes reflection in the form of sharing individual and corporate experiences of God, as a summary of what God has been doing and saying to the church family. During our Eucharist service at Post Green, quite soon after the beginning one of the worship leaders asks, 'Well, what has God been doing in our life this week.' This reflection is a stabilising factor and gives support to a child's personal experience of God and her sense of being among people who know God.

SKILLS FOR COMMUNICATION

As in relationships with other people, a relationship with God requires the skills of communication, verbal and non-verbal. Tools for communication are developed into skills through experience with others, in their relationships with God. Worship is the context of relationship to God, whether individual or corporate. Many of the tools are similar.

Speaking and listening to God in a variety of ways is prayer. It is learned in several ways. Often in our Community Eucharist, when Hannah has something to tell everyone, she falters and then gets Sue, her mother, to say it as she wants it. In our older children we see a growing confidence and skill in presenting their own testimonies.

Times of testimony and prayer are supportive to a child's experiencing and learning. With us, each of the children sits with an adult who will help her present her testimony or prayer. This is sometimes preceded by quietly explaining what is happening in the group, or by the child's explaining to the adult her concern. In the context of the service the adult, by example and encouragement, helps the child grow in her ability to participate actively.

Through its service structure or liturgy the church family can make this participation possible, through making open times of testimony and simple prayers, deeply expressive of God's life but simple in form. A profound experience is not denied by the inclusion of children in the service, even though simpler forms are used.

Listening is part of communication. My relationship with God involves a lot of listening. It is two way or it is not a mature relationship. My child's relationship to me requires her to listen.

All communication in relationships requires both persons to talk and listen. So the listening in worship is active listening for God to speak to us. How he speaks helps us know how to listen, and how to help our children listen.

Part of our expecting God to speak to all of us together is to listen to him together. As a Community we, therefore, work on helping children to listen with us. If we expect God to speak only to the adults we should not require the children to listen; their merely being quiet is no good to them, and if this is our only requirement or expectation of them we might as well send them to another location where they will not distract us. However, if we expect God to speak to all of us together, as well he might since we are all his family gathered, it is worth all of us listening together.

How does God speak in verbal forms? This happens in a clear way through such means as preaching, teaching, testimony, prophecy and interpretation of tongues. The parent or adult with each baby or child can expect the child to listen, and can encourage or require listening. The person speaking will know that children are listening for God's word, so will tend to speak more briefly and simply, without changing the truth or strength of the content. Simple language is a communication form, a language, not an adaptation of the importance or strength of the word of God.

Obviously such listening is a skill to be learned by example, experience and positive discipline. Here is how we regularly introduce our babies and young children to active listening.

We start at home, rather than in the big crowd at church. At a regular time, for example at prayers and/or a bible story after a meal, the whole family participates, speaking and listening to each other. The baby held by an adult is encouraged in whispers, 'Listen, David is telling us something. What is he saying?' At first she listens only for moments but is quiet even for several minutes. When she yells and drowns out everyone else, we take her out of the room saying gently, 'When Lisa is ready to listen we will come back.' Then we come back when we feel Lisa may be quiet a bit longer.

The concept of listening for these few minutes is soon learned, especially if the routine is kept up every day. Talk about this with the rest of the family, even other young children, so they understand what the baby is learning. The activity of listening can be learned in a few weeks even by a one year old. Support their listening by using bible story books with pictures, and testimonies with models or examples. Be tolerant of fretful times, and do not punish. Treat this as a group time with the baby learning to be a member of the group rather than being a naughty distraction. It is her wanting to be with everyone that will motivate her to listen, and her being with everyone will become enjoyable to all.

It is apparent, too, that the child, who really only learns through experience, will be aware of God only as adults are aware of him. At family prayer time we share the reality of our relationship with God, including our sorrows and joy, so that the children are aware of the reality of God's receiving these. We do not limit the time to presenting helpful information or knowledgeable prayers. It is an opening up of real life worked out with God.

We now transfer this listening to the church. At first a child will not be able to listen for very long. But just like at home, I use the approach of 'Let's go out till you are ready to listen.' This has two purposes. The child discovers that she does want to be part of what is happening, part of the family she enjoys. Also, if small children are making noise whenever they wish, drowning things out, then there is nothing for anyone to listen to; the words of God are drowned out. Participation in listening actively to God does require that everyone tries to expect and listen to his word.

Other church members can support at this point. They are not angry with the child or wish her to be punished. We find ways to help the adult or parent who has the child, such as giving them a seat at the end of the row so going out is easier. Those leading the service can use visual illustrations and forms so the child, whose comprehension is limited, can be involved. I also encourage those with very small children, despite the risk of noise, to sit at the front or wherever is the best place for seeing what is happening. Then the risk of noise actually becomes less.

Do not expect a congregation to endlessly accept a shouting child who is not learning to listen. The word of God is vital to life. If you do not want the child to learn active listening, or it is inappropriate in your church, make other arrangements. Continual noise from children, which is not a stage of learning, and which prevents other members being able to participate will result in separate services for those with children and those without. A worship gathering for the whole church family will be almost impossible.

What of non-verbal communication with God. How will I feel that I have told God I love him, and how will a child feel this? Chiefly the forms of communication that are non-verbal are those that are expressive of senses and emotions. The music of the service, for instance, as it is offered to God, often expresses feelings to him, as well as having verbal content. The music itself carries a feeling. Children often get very involved in and responsive to the church's hymns and songs, long before being able to read. I recently stood next to a nine year old as we worshipped with 'Crown Him with many crowns, the Lamb upon His throne'. The strength of the hymn for him lay more in the majesty and splendour than in the detailed meaning of the words.

If the congregation includes non-verbal forms of worship, children can participate actively in a profound experience of God. Posture, and dance, can express my love and feelings to God. I can speak to him without words. Postures, not just the submissive one of kneeling with bowed head (though this is fine), can include hands raised in prayer or song, ways of standing and sitting, 'actions' with songs. 'We love the Lord', a song from *Sound of Living Waters*, has actions that express such worship to God. Dance that includes the whole congregation touches the child more than a performance.

Colours used in worship can be an expression of both the individual and the congregation to God. Our excitement and joy at the life he gives can be expressed in decorations, whether banners or vestments. The same means can be used to express our sorrow and repentance.

To feel that God loves us, both the children and most of the rest of us require a tactile experience, something we can touch or taste. For example, the hug or similar greeting during the Peace gives this message. So, too, in a very particular way does the receiving of bread and wine. These are received by us in all of our senses as gifts of God's life to us, expressions of his love. Alongside this, the way we listen to, greet and encourage one another supports our feeling that God has received us.

This all goes to say that participation with the whole of ourselves, body and mind, is involved in deep communication with God. There is experience as well as information, which brings integrated knowledge of him. The involvement of the whole congregation in this experience is the context for the child to grow in relationship to God in worship.

There can be a tendency for us adults to think that children cannot actively take part unless the worship skips along quite swiftly. This, however, can run counter to their experiencing awe and wonder in God's presence, or adequately responding to a sense of majesty. With some help from the adult she is with, the child may learn to be attentive during the silence in which some aspects of worship are expressed. It is a step or so on from listening actively to another person's voice, yet possible.

Learning the tools of worship, as with the learning of skills in other relationships, involves being in the presence of those who are using them with skill, and who make an opening for the young ones to use those tools till they too become skilful.

CELEBRATION

When children have reached the age when belonging to a group is exciting to them, their sense of God and their worship grows. They will now be at the stage of joint projects in play, and will enjoy group activities such as family outings. The individual child has a sense of what the group is and of her own belonging to it. She is fairly confident in presenting herself with and without words, readily listens to others, is beginning to recognise and understand and feel for others.

The child is still dependent on the whole church family for her relationship to God and is ready for further growth. It is as if, from the security of being a person in the group, perceiving the identity of others and the identity of the group, the child is now ready to be involved in corporate challenge and adventure, within the setting of the whole church. In this, there is a coming together of experience and information, of daily life and God's word, of doctrine and practice. The child can now sense and perceive the great festivals of the church. As the church lives out the confession and repentance of Lent the child will be touched and drawn into this repentance. Or there is the growing sense of excitement of joy in Advent, and the majesty of Easter. These are not only festivals to celebrate history or general truths. Rather, they are celebrations of life lived and worked out with God. Often they have been celebrated throughout church history, just as we celebrate our joy at God's redemption of us, at Easter.

As the church through its daily experience of God recognises and responds to his concerns, the inclusion of these in worship feeds the child in her relationship to God.

God gave us a very deep love for our friend Gershom Nyaronga during his time with us, a deep sense of commitment to him and his ministry. Throughout the friendship, our children have been part of working out our gifts to him. When we include prayer for Gershom in our worship times the children have readily taken part in them. Similarly, as we have fasted or celebrated, our children have been included as appropriate. In our dealing with God they have seen reality.

In our ongoing grappling with the understanding of peace issues, Richard, aged six, went with a group to discover what was happening at Greenham Common. It gave him a very tangible sense of involvement in our struggles to understand ourselves as peacemakers and gave him yet another way to see our commitment to God's word in its daily outworking. He listened and questioned and responded.

As we, as God's family, work at the integration of daily life and worship our children experience the challenges of Christian life and ministry. The adventures, the mistakes, the joys and sorrows are open to their participation. The child grows in her sense of knowing God as she takes full part in the life we live with him. She gets to know his voice and how we know it is him speaking. She takes part in our corporate confession, repentance, renewal, faithfulness, praise and responsibility.

The ways she is helped and grows employ all the tools and skills we have mentioned: the active participation in church worship, the family worship, the time to reflect alone and with a parent. Out of all this she will begin to recognise the nature of God, the reality of him and his life. She will connect prayer with testimony, will recognise a faithful response to God's word, will know the Spirit is working among his people. Her own approach to God, while still tentative, can then have a sense of depth and definite experience.

Children should also have some involvement in sorting out what God's word means in everyday practical situations. It helps if young people can be around as other members of the church are considering and working out what God's word means to them.

PERSONAL RESPONSIBILITY

When children reach an age of becoming responsible for

many of their own choices, this finds expression in the church. Or does it? The young adult becomes responsible for her own relationship to God. She has reached an age where she sticks at it through friendship problems and is beginning to understand what committed friendships are. She can now consider a committed relationship with God. She knows who he is, and is now working this out herself, not just because her family lives this way.

At this point a young adult should be able to see her involvement in the church as that of a responsible member, partly because she wants to be in charge of her own life with God. She will present her own needs and requests, pursue her own friendships, and so on. She can become an adult member of the church, as it has committed itself to become the kingdom of heaven on earth. Our growing young people must have access to this responsibility, for without it they will not grow to maturity. They must have opportunity for responsibility in the areas of their gifts and talents, everything from administration to music, caring and labouring. The maturing of the person with God ties in with the growing and maturing experience of him. The broad responsibility of life in Christ, God's life in us, is handed to the young adult to develop to her fullest potential.

CHOICES ABOUT THE EUCHARIST

Over the recent years, many thousands of people have visited Post Green Community, both in our homes and at our camps. A high point of many of these visits has been the Eucharist and the way in which everyone takes part, adults and children alike. All are received, all worship and all receive the bread and wine. For us, all of our children belong to the family of God's people here. None of them are outsiders. For us, the Eucharist is both an expression of our corporate life and a sacrament of grace. The bread and the wine are means of grace that the child needs as much as the adult. Each time a child goes from here to face the world, in school or in town, she needs the grace of God to know who she is – his child.

This is a current area of question in many churches. Much of the resolution of the issue will lie in understanding God's relationship to the child before she reaches an age of being personally accountable for her life, or even before understanding the theology of life.

Section Five

THE CHURCH IS THE FAMILY

Chapter 9
A WAY OF LIVING

> Your kingdom come, your will be done,
> Now that we have become your sons.
> Let the prayer of our hearts daily be:
> God, make us your family.
>
> **Tim Whipple**

Traditionally throughout history, the family has found its support and focus in a local community. Here it has had a context that has made the family viable. I believe the family is only going to be a viable unit as it functions within the larger local community. There are many factors essential to life, which will help the child grow, that cannot be provided by the small family unit alone. Nor could they be provided by a return to the 'extended family' that is so often quoted as belonging to previous generations, for society has evolved beyond that stage. In the family in ages past, not only did blood relatives give support, emotional and other, but the community also gave life through its worship focus, celebrations, discipline, work and other structures. There were many shortcomings, and it would be romantic to think otherwise, but industrialisation and urbanisation have reduced the effectiveness of all forms of community life.

The significance of the local church has disintegrated with this development. While some people still retain some nominal links with the church, using it for weddings, baptisms and burials, there is now a far lower percentage of active churchgoing in Britain than for instance in Russia, a country that is so often decried as God-less and even anti-Christ. The church is no longer the head of the local community. The village celebrations which in some areas survive were free and easy times where children could run around among the people. Everyone knew each other, so the children were safe. These days, there are sometimes local celebrations, essentially money-making, that provide some focus. Many, however, are now so great in numbers that people are de-personalised and you meet no one you know.

Work structures, especially in cities and conurbations, separate and isolate individuals. Very often the people living in one street do not work together. Nor is there opportunity for children to see where their parents work or what they do, and they can never experience working alongside them or other adults. They do not have patterns or models around them, except perhaps teachers or housewives. They have little or no opportunity to work with a group of people on a project. No one, however, can stem the tide of time and history, nor would they necessarily want to.

GOD'S PEOPLE – A COMMUNITY WITH A HEART

What of the essential needs of the child in the family? Who will meet them? There has been a history within the church of God's people living in small, local communities, close-knit groups, not necessarily blood related. These provided not only the essential factors mentioned above, but also focused on the principles of God's kingdom. The heart of such a community is focused on God, and the social and other needs of the children within their families are met. What kinds of work can a community of God's people undertake, and in what ways can children be involved in these? What events are celebrated together and how can they best be celebrated?

WORSHIP

The local church, a community of God's people, will see its purpose, its heart, its life and expression centred on God. The worshipping response to this finds practical expression in the church's life. Times of worship will include responses to God about all aspects of the community's life, both current and potential.

An example: Today, as I write this, is a General Election, a fact of great importance for our everyday life. The government has a significant effect on the state of our everyday life, so as Christians we are very concerned with the outcome. Therefore, this week our Community included in its worship a summary of election factors, including how each party's manifesto relates to Christian principles. Last week some of our children spontaneously held their own election. They filled out ballot papers as well as writing a manifesto. It may have been a game but for them it was a significant step in discovering their own priorities.

The local church will find itself inextricably implicated in national affairs that are clearly not based on Jesus' life principles. These are issues like British wealth compared with Third World poverty, spending on defence compared with aid to children in poverty, or the unemployed, ecological considerations, and so on. There will be times of repentance of corporate sin.

Another example of daily life: Just recently at Post Green we had a special time during our Eucharist service to share the good things God has done for us during a time of financial pressure, and to thank him for them. We thanked him for the gifts of money. We also heard of some other good things like visiting our Swap Shop (the place where we keep our second-hand clothing) and finding just the shoes needed. There was great excitement, as one household had received a box of second-hand clothes which included summer clothes for the children.

There will also be times of thanksgiving for events in the area, as they affect the church family; for aspects of education, the local council, elections, campaigns and local help projects like the Samaritans. There will be times of thanksgiving that are similar to the harvest services of rural communities, for food and clothing.

The great events of Jesus' life and ministry will be celebrated in worship: his birth, his death, his resurrection. These will be focal points in the church's life. How can our children feel the significance of Jesus' birth? Let us have a celebration that is not crowded out with spending money, over-eating, fairy tales.

For a long time a particular myth has controlled parents, saying subtly that although they cannot make the whole of life perfect for their child they *can* make Christmas perfect. So they have to give just the right present.

I sometimes get looks of horror as I tell people that there have been Christmases or birthdays when I have spent no money on Jacqueline. Yet never has she been without a gift I have been very happy to give to her. Our life has shown us the value of a gift made by the giver. I knit, mostly with recycled wool, and grow houseplants, and make lots of other small gifts.

It is great fun when our worship life includes and affirms such renewed attitudes and responses to life, in thanksgiving to God for his provision.

FESTIVITY

In the local church, as a small community, the child can experience celebrating life. There is a social expression of life in Christ, focussed in worship. As with a wedding, first a contract is made before God in the context of serious yet joyful worship. This is followed by a 'social' celebration, food and dancing. So, too, with other events of community life.

Through these the fun, excitement, humour and joys of family life are shared. There is also the expression of grief, as when funerals happen. These are the community or local church's experiences in which children can share. There is friendly involvement with a larger small family. A break from ordinary life gives room for the expression of many kinds of feelings. Bank holidays, for instance, can be spent at outings, fêtes or other friendly gatherings.

Last summer my household invited the rest of our Community to a fête in our garden. Each family or household brought a stall. Nobody charged any money. We rolled tennis balls into buckets, threw darts, ran races, painted pictures, looked at a stall of family antiques, guessed whose baby photo was whose and many more activities. There was lots of laughter, and every one who entered a race got a prize and the spectators ate up all the spare prize sweets.

Fêtes and carnivals are events that can be dominated by fierce competition and lots of money. But a congregation can play down the money-making aspect and have fun together. It is better to put fund-raising under another category, with work or stewardship campaigns.

Local community celebrations have been much affected by television. For example, the day of the Royal Wedding of Charles and Diana was spent by many in front of the television set. Of course the television helped us 'see' what happened, but those who turned out onto the streets felt the enormous excitement of being part of a great crowd celebrating together.

The church can look at the events of its own life, both in the local area and nationally, and so consider a full programme for its family life. Harvest suppers, for instance, are good for the whole church family to enjoy together. It can be organised and catered for centrally, everyone can buy tickets to contribute to the costs. In our own Community, however, we have found more satisfaction if every individual and family has made something for the common meal. Some do savouries, some do sweets, and so on. Everyone, including the children, brings something and so has the satisfaction of knowing he has contributed to the celebration.

A common meal is also a way for the church family to celebrate Christmas together. If the church family wants to help lonely people over Christmas a meal of this kind with games and fun is a good way to include everyone. Here at Post Green, for instance, we had a married couple living with us who taught us Square Dancing on some very enjoyable evenings. During the winter, or even on a summer evening outside, it is also fun to have a barn dance. Lots of country dances are very simple and even quite young children can join in. Lots of schools still teach traditional country dances, and it is amazing how easily everyone can catch on to those based on a simple skipping step.

The talents of the church family are part of our entertainment. Pantomimes can be adapted to fit various levels of skill and various numbers of participants. A professional script is not always helpful, often being too long for our amateur actors and children. Often a church member has either adapted or written a script that suits the family better. It is great fun to see members of our own family dressed up and entertaining us. The children love such productions whether they are in the cast or the audience.

Another favourite can be a concert. Lots of members take part in the programme, which is a mixture of all sorts of offerings: music (both classical and folk), readings from favourite authors or from personal writing, drama and skits. We find among ourselves a Master of Ceremonies who can link the pieces together and organise the programme.

Can Mothering Sunday become a celebration of family life in the church, a celebration for all, not just some of the congregation? The church can reconsider many traditional celebrations, to re-emphasise the family's gathering for fun together. It is very worthwhile having celebrations for fun, rather than for the financial reasons that seem to be such an important factor so often.

WORK

When a family works together on a project there is a great

sense of common satisfaction at its completion. Such activity also gives opportunity for children to be doing various types of significant family work alongside adults. They can learn skills from various people as well as experience that different adults tackle projects in different, but equally acceptable, ways.

An example from our life: Early each year Robert King, our Community Administrator, gives us a list of dates for 'Work Days'. These are Saturdays set aside by the whole Community to get our commerical caravan site ready for opening on April 1st, as well as preparing our camp site for our summer camps. We all turn out in our oldest jeans and jumpers (one March workday was interrupted by flurries of snow). We gather and form into working groups, including the children, to sweep and dig, to scrub and paint. We put up signs, repair winter damage, prune and trim edges and hedges.

In the context of these friendly contacts with a working environment, attitudes to work will be established. Since all of us expect to earn our living for a large number of years, such a friendly introduction for our children to various jobs is helpful.

It may be unusual for church members to work together or even near each other. So many jobs are now so distant from home that most people have to commute. In the places where we are buyers or users of services we meet mostly strangers. Do find ways for children to experience their parents and other church members at work, be it the car mechanic, shop assistant, electrician, secretary, computer operator. See if a church member will show your child round, and introduce him to the job as a friend. This will help him as he grows to have a picture of what earning a living and job satisfaction can mean. Similarly, other mothers may invite your child around for a morning to help with housework and young children. From such contact a child can get a real impression of job possibilities, not depending simply on brochures and verbal information.

There are also opportunities within the life of the church for adults and children to work together. Often these are habitually done by adults, and some rethinking may be necessary.

The church building is cleaned, polished and decorated. Instead of this being a weekday job, could this be done on Saturday so families with children can help from time to time? Paired up with an adult, not necessarily his parent, each child can work on a particular chore, like sweeping up, tidying and dusting bookshelves, arranging flowers, cleaning brass and silver, laundering cloths and vestments. There may be the occasional projects like folding and stapling the parish newsletter, delivering notices door-to-door, preparing for special services. The church I attend has a special work project to prepare candles and oranges for a Christingle service each Christmas time. All these, with some advance thought, can include children.

There will be work around the church that is not particularly related to the worship services. Lawn mowing and other gardening, building maintenance and repairs all require attention. With this kind of work a child may be interested in helping regularly in one particular area, as for instance the garden.

When there is a church family celebration, plan it in such a way that children can help in the work and fun of both preparation and clearing up.

We recently had a day for thinking over our life and purpose as a Community. Our children had their own group, first writing and painting about their thoughts on why God has us living this way. Then I spent the afternoon with them, helping them cook pizzas for the whole Community (eighty people). About twenty children aged three to fifteen joined in mixing and rolling, spreading sauce and cheese, sprinkling on an assortment of toppings. With the help of two adults who organised a bit, and two teenagers who saw all the pizzas through the oven stage, they made a delicious meal. Dessert was easier. They served us ice-cream in wafers. Their sense of satisfaction and self-esteem was enormous.

An event to which each feels he has contributed something of value is enjoyed by all, thus affirming each person's contribution. To be a 'receiver' of good things is only half of friendship, the other being to know how and what to give. Children can work on cooking, table setting, arranging chairs, welcoming, general planning, cleaning and sweeping, washing up, serving. Some children are able to lead games or activities.

Doing jobs around the church can include working both with people and with things. Cleaning and tidying mean working with things, handing out books involves being friendly to others. Offer children times for both kinds of work. They require different attitudes and approach. Dealing with things involves efficiency and order, and brooms and brushes stay where you put them. Dealing with people involves being ready to change and adapt whatever plans we have made, in order to meet the needs of the person who arrives.

As children grow, I find it increasingly important for them

to experience chores they do not want to do at first. In our family, no one *likes* washing up. But we all know it is a necessary chore. And the children help on a rota basis. Part of becoming a responsible member of society is learning to do the necessary family work, not only when we 'feel like doing it'. Positive attitudes to regular family chores are learned alongside adults who, knowing the necessity, get on and enjoy doing them. A false picture is built if children are regularly excused or never given work they do not like.

Whatever kinds of work a child has been doing, a most important aspect of job satisfaction lies in the person himself being pleased with it. It is good to say, 'Are you pleased with what you have done?' Be glad with them. If they are not, see if you can help. Avoid judging the child's effort or deciding for him whether he has enjoyed it. A similar good question would be, 'Have you enjoyed yourself?' and find out what he thinks. In other words, reflect on the job with your child, thus creating with him a way to look forward to his own growth in skills and responsibility.

CREATIVITY

The church can be a place for everyone to develop his creativity. The gifts and talents of each person will be varied. Many find expression for themselves in arts and activities, some in administration and organisation, some in reading and study. All can be expressed with care and consideration and in service to others.

Within the church's life and worship there has always been lots of musical expression. It has not always fallen into the categories of choir, organist and congregation. In fact, music can be an opening for other creativity. In church services a small orchestra or band can help lead the worship. Children could be in a choir for special occasions.

Several times now our Sunday School children have rehearsed recorder and percussion parts to hymns and songs and then played them in our church services. Our organist is now planning to form a small orchestra to accompany our worship. He is going to include children as well as adults.

When people have other musical gifts and interests, include them in a concert or entertainment at a party. Here the individual or family can make music for others to listen to and enjoy. Similarly, a small band could play pieces that would never fit into worship services. A skilled musician, like a music teacher, may be able to arrange parts in such a way that many levels of skill may be brought together in the band.

Some church buildings lend themselves to having large wall-hangings or banners. These can illustrate or summerise a teaching point or worship response. Develop the ideas of adults and children and work together on design and construction. Our own Sunday School has often hung a huge banner in the church, basing it on the present teaching theme. Then the whole church become aware of and involved in our work.

If your church is one that includes dance in worship, have you included dance styles through which men and children can enjoy and express themselves? Some more ballet type dances seem suited only to people of particular shape and stature. Folk dance lends itself more readily to a variety of people in the church family.

Children's gifts in organisation can find expression, too. The rotas, work projects and general 'office' work of a church all require practical organisation. Can adults and children work together on these, after school or at weekends?

One exciting way of being creative together has been, for our church, a Christmas Workshop Day. With several organisers planning together, a few adults and lots of children have spent a Saturday together making Christmas presents, cards and calendars. This year we also made puppets, leather purses, pencil cases and we dipped candles. It has been good getting to know each other in this way, and fun making attractive presents for very little cost.

Many churches have successfully run Holiday Play Programmes. While these are a benefit to children who otherwise might have little or no chance for creative play, they can also offer opportunity for adults and children of the church to be together. There are many adults who can find time to come to a play programme to share their own particular skill or hobby with a group of three or four children.

THE CHURCH'S CARING, HELPING AND REACHING OUT

In ministry the church family steps outside itself to offer the life of Christ to the world. This takes many forms, including evangelism and serving. In some ways the church is 'as a light set on a hill'. The presence of God's people attracts others from outside. Visitors and new people come to receive life. Often their patterns of relationships, of understanding, of self-image, speak more of the world than the kingdom. Often new families have unhelpful ways of relating to each other. These can effect the church and the children quite considerably.

Children may grab things from others, may hit other children or generally behave in a disruptive way. Those already established in the church family's way may need lots of encouragement to remain tolerant and accepting of such a newcomer. Only gradually will this child and new family learn the ways of the kingdom as expressed in the particular customs of any one church. Similarly, a new child may be withdrawn or shy and confused in the new place. Some special attention may be needed to get him involved and happy. In all these circumstances the children of the church are in contact with the church's ministry and will feel its weight. As far as possible help them to understand and help newcomers. Ask a child, for example, to help new people find their way round.

Children very soon see the difference between church life and life in many schools. In a way that is normally unprotected they are being challenged by the systems of the world, through competition and often failure. Most children can adapt to this, can work with the differences. The difficulties do not overwhelm the affirming experience of home and church. But every child needs help and encouragement. Time to talk – reflection – is essential if the children are to remain positive. With such help children may want or may be able to carry consideration and care into the everyday environment at school.

A child, being a dependent member of God's family, cannot carry the responsibility for serving God in a particular role. Alongside a responsible adult member, however, he will help. This means that where a child is doing a responsible job in the church's life he knows which adult member will always help him if there is difficulty. If the problem cannot be readily sorted out, the adult will make sure it is followed through. Similarly, if the church leaders feel the job is not being done as they would like, this responsible adult and the child will sort it out together. If the child is not able to do his part, if, for instance, he is ill, the adult will take responsibility. This may sound complicated, but a child alone cannot be responsible for ministry because he is not yet a committed adult member. He can only be involved with those who are.

When she was very young my daughter found that she really enjoyed visiting several old age pensioners who lived near us. They enjoyed her company and she loved to hear them talk of times gone by, getting out their old photos and mementoes. It resulted in long-standing friendships. This all began when my mother was a home-help and she took Jacqueline with her. Soon she wanted to visit whether my mother went or not. That began when she was three. Such friendly chats over a cup of tea affirm both people. Often older people are lonely because they are housebound, not because they are unfriendly.

It has always been delightful to have our children and teenagers help us when a Fisherfolk team goes out to other places. Jacqueline was in a Christmas play in a Blandford church; one of the boys was in a play in Wareham, and lots have helped us with dances. One six-year-old has played his bongo drum regularly at camps, next to an adult drummer.

The ongoing life of the church, maintaining itself and going out to others, can include every member. For in the togetherness is learning and affirmation as well as a secure and viable context for the life of the families and their children. However, unless the church is prepared to become pastorally concerned for the development of the whole human person, to fullness in all its aspects and not just the religious or spiritual, it will not be a community that nurtures the life of children.

Chapter 10
'OF SUCH IS THE KINGDOM OF HEAVEN'

It's not who borned you that matters
but who loves you.

International Year of the Child Handbook

The church is the body of Christ in the world. Among God's people the life of Christ is lived, expressing his concerns, his attitudes, his awareness of God. Included in this is his attitude to children. He is the one who blessed them and pointed out that his disciples could learn from them.

The affirmation and value that Jesus gave to several oppressed groups, including the poor and women, was unusual for his time. So, too, was his attitude to children. Yet undoubtedly he saw them as people for whom the kingdom of heaven had a special concern.

How will the child of today be received and cared for by the church? Since we are similar to the world around us we, like the disciples, might send away the children and their mothers. In our minds we may rationalise this and think, 'Come to us when you are responsible adults and can understand.' In our hearts we may even doubt our ability to recognise or meet their needs.

But turning to a faithful response, how will we, the family of God, receive and nurture the families and the children among us? How will we take hold of the life in us and offer it to the children so that they will feel loved and affirmed and be nurtured?

In us will be the intention to so affirm each child that when she reaches the stage of responsibility for herself, of independence, she will know what it will mean to choose God's life for herself. For me, to choose God's life felt like a step in the dark, but for the child who has grown in an awareness of God there is a greater sense of ease in doing this. What is involved?

The church will first acknowledge that the child belongs to the family. Symbolic of this is the baptism and naming: this can be a meaningful action on the part of the whole church family as well as the smaller family. It can be undertaken in such a way that the congregation feels and thinks, 'This is our child.' Not only through godparents and the family will the needs of the child be considered. There will be within the church a sense of family that affirms the personhood of all members and receives the child in its midst. The church's heart will be open and active toward children. There will be ongoing interest in the child from the various members and an active concern for the child's whole life.

FOCUS FOR MINISTRY TO CHILDREN

The active concern for children in the church will normally be expressed by an individual or group who have a special interest in them. This is not simply a parents group. Just as many of our churches have groups who focus on and administrate areas such as pastoral care, worship or fund raising, so there will be one whose area is concern for children. In our Community this group functions like a bridge between the family and the various facets of the church's life, so that in all aspects there is an awareness of the child and her family. This means that if something new ought to happen in terms of the children's growth and the support they need, this group will make proposals and present them in the necessary places. If a particular decision would affect the child and the family negatively, this group would point that out, too. Where principles should be reconsidered in the light of children's needs the group would draw attention to them. Similarly, they would challenge any situation in which a child was being treated unjustly or was oppressed, and would speak out for the rights of children and for their needs being met fully.

In other words, children and their families become an area of ministry concern in the body of Christ, a ministry whose concern is the fullness and wholeness of life.

There are a number of significant areas to be considered.

OPPORTUNITIES FOR CONTACT, FELLOWSHIP AND FRIENDSHIP

Does the child have sufficient opportunity for contact, fellowship and friendship?

On informal occasions in our life the child can get to know adults other than parents. Through celebration, work and worship the child can become acquainted with a variety of people, people she might not normally contact, like teenagers, old people, single people.

The difference between the church members and those outside the church, is that the church members have chosen the Christian faith. In her parents a child experiences two Christian adults and the way they work out their faith. Through the church she will experience other married couples, single parents, single adults, widowed and divorced people, old and young and people of other races and cultures. All of these are in their own way living out the Christian faith. The picture of Christian lifestyle is broadened in the child's experience.

In a lively church the child can find friendship with other children whose families are working on Christian principles. There will be many similarities, and there is fellowship for the child. For example, there will be other children who are encouraged not to fight, are encouraged to care for others. They may feel difficulties in understanding such principles in their school lives, and conversation helps.

It is a normal human characteristic to choose friendship with people similar to ourselves. We choose a housing estate, for instance, where things are our style, and so are the people. We tend to mix socially with those like us and encourage our children at school to choose friends with similar values. The church is often a place of fellowship between many walks of life, a place for befriending those unlike us and a place, therefore, for our children to widen their value systems.

TO PERCEIVE THE CHURCH

Significant to the biblical teaching on the Eucharist is the concept of perceiving the body of Christ. What opportunities are there for the child to perceive Christ's body, the church?

Worship is one situation where this can happen. At the

weekly worship service the child will look around and see many familiar faces. These are the people who come together with a common purpose and commitment, who brings their worship offering and allegiance to God and express them corporately. The child becomes aware of those who lead, those who serve, those who laugh and are friendly, those who are serious. In being part of this group and the relationships within it the child will intuitively and experientially get a perception of the body of Christ: that which is everyone together. In this the child will perceive the meaning of the Eucharist itself, what it means in this group. She will also be aware of relationships, of reverence and any other common attitudes present.

Like a family, each church family will have its own ways of being informal together. What it does will be characteristic of its life. Some of the church groups who have come to Post Green camps over the years have identifiable and characteristic ways of being together. In them the child perceives the body of Christ, sensing the spirit of the group. The styles of greeting, the attitudes to individuals, the forms of expression, the language used are all apparent. Affection and touch, caring and sharing will all be visible to the child, as they are part of this life.

As the church works together the child will see its purpose and attitudes, and discover the balance between the person and the function, between getting the job done and the fun of being together.

Through being part of and aware of the body of Christ, the child will perceive the meaning and identity of this family of God's people.

What do our children see as they are part of our church? Do they see the principles of the kingdom of heaven at work, the body of Christ active? Does the child experience a family that actively cares for its members or does she mainly see a Sundays-only caring?

This perception will also affect the child's eventual decision about choosing to follow Christ. 'If I choose to follow the Christian faith, my life will probably be something like this. Is that what I want?' A group who cares for the interests of children will concern itself with such perception.

TO CONSIDER ALL ASPECTS OF CHILD CARE

Do the children of the church have a sense of belonging, of

identity in the church? And does the church have a sense of the children being 'ours'?

The structure of the church's life may need to be reconsidered for this two-way sense of belonging to become a reality.

It is easy for the small, natural family to be the only common ground for child and church. Consider baptism and the timing of it. When can all the regular committed members of the congregation to present to assert that this child is ours? An effective place for Baptism is during one of the church's main services.

Next, consider the godparents or sponsors. Friendship with the parents is probably less important than that these people represent to the child the church to which they belong. In other words, these are the adults who are concerned for the life of this child *in the church* and will work to keep the child and her family closely within the church's care. Additionally, the church, through the group that makes children its particular concern, could help in choosing godparents.

Many parents have only such knowledge of child development as they glean from their own parents. Many Sunday School teachers repeat the ways they themselves learned. There are now a number of courses available that could be used by parents and other adults to learn about child development. Courses about children in the church are also becoming more available. Many of these help adults reconsider styles of parenting to suit the present situation. A study group of adults may be formed, much as a bible study group is. In this context members could follow the study material and also talk over their personal questions and interests. The particular opportunities there are for each child to develop fully can be looked into. Can the church family help fill the gaps in any child's experience, in education or play?'

How does each child manage in friendships with other church members? Does she have the necessary support and help?

Are the children of the church growing to their full potential, discovering their own creativity and giftedness?

What opportunities for responsibility are offered to each child, at every age and stage? The structure of life in the church can include this, with scope for personal choice and approach. Of all areas of growth this is the one that is least supported in the traditional structures of most churches.

What of the handicapped child who has particular needs and can often be very wearing on parents? Is her need considered within the church?

The child's spiritual growth is another area of concern. Is there an environment in which the child has time to experience and sense who God is, his power, his love, his friendship and his concerns? Are those who lead children – parents, Sunday School teachers, worship leaders – introducing the child to God?

In what aspects of the church's worship life can the child discover and offer her own responses to God? This may happen in a children's group, in the small, natural family or in the main worship services; hopefully in all three.

Along with all members of the church, are children becoming aware of their own roots and history as God's people? There is biblical history and the history of the church through the ages. As God's people we have forebears, heroes or heroines of our faith, whom you will not find mentioned in school, for example, where history is more concerned with national and political figures. The saints of the church have fascinating and encouraging testimonies and teaching to offer us.

Through what means, at home or church, are children learning the principles of the kingdom, biblical teaching? This learning will come through experience and understanding, as appropriate to their ages and stages.

TO INTERPRET THE CHILD AND THE CHURCH TO ONE ANOTHER

There has been general change in attitude towards children. Society, as represented in the education system, has changed. But its changes, though valid, are often misunderstood by parents and older generations.

That old maxim 'Children should be seen and not heard' is an example. We now want to *listen*.

The family of the church, many of those members grew up with the old understanding of children, can bar opportunity to work constructively with new attitudes and approaches. Teaching in the church, through small groups, at main services or individually, can focus on the ways in which God is speaking to his people, not just giving instruction but offering understanding and empathy for those to whom the principles are new. In this way the principles will become part of the understanding and experience of church leaders, and can in turn be taught to other church members.

Those with special concern for children will begin to live out renewed attitudes, and this will help teach alongside the words. For example, those who lead worship can include the concerns and expression of children, facilitating their involvement. Those who plan music can include hymns and songs that are inclusive of children.

There will be times of misunderstanding. The 'generation gap' often seen between teenagers and adults is often the result of misunderstanding. The world of the older generation was a different one from the one young people deal with. Language is different, pressures and customs are different, education and peer group influences, all are different. They make for a gap in understanding. The group with a concern for children can help interpret the groups to one another, standing in this gap, so tolerance and care can grow among the members of the church. Such interpretation can support young people through what seems to them an age of great stress.

THE INTERESTS OF ALL CHILDREN

Over the next few years several significant social factors will bear fruit in the quality of life of society in general.

Elements of life such as divorce rates, numbers of single parents, children in care, family breakdown and unemployment rates, poverty levels are affecting the life of children in society and the church. Many of these factors are just as real in the church as outside. Many aspects of life for all children will be affected. Along with the positive understanding of the child as a person will come a breaking down of the structures that normally protect her.

Yet children do not have a voice to cry for help.

Statistics may floor us with the size of this problem, worldwide. We may or may not sense our ability to make any difference.

The church does have a call to, as well as a reputation for, caring for the poor and the oppressed. Many publications, many prophets, are calling the church to be active in love for children. In the British Council of Churches booklet *Child in the Church* we are asked. 'How can we be Christian with our children?' rather than, 'How can we make our children Christian?'

Erin Pizzey, in *The Sunday Times* (11 October 1981), wrote

of the dream of a generation of parents in the Sixties, a dream with some similarities to our own. These parents dreamed of an egalitarian society, caring and humane, and they reaped a fruit they had not planned:

The ideal of the comprehensive system was beautifully conceived, but . . . it did not allow for the reality of the greedy, self-serving nature of the human animal. The idea was that when children from all walks of life met together in their thousands . . . they would with one accord all rise to the top like cream and share with each other the best of their experiences . . . most of the children sank to the bottom like stones.

She noted some success: 'They are confident, classless and much kinder than we were. They are all much closer to their parents. . . . That part of the dream has come true.'

I have a dream.

I recognise the truth in Erin Pizzey's statements, but as a child of God I have another, bigger dream. I want to see and always work for the kingdom of heaven.

Through the pages of history parts of society have recognised that no man may own another man. So there came an end to slavery. Through the last one hundred years women have begun to claim the right to be persons in the structures of society, responsible, mature members. In the foreseeable future there may be laws to protect women from the kind of 'ownership' that turns a blind eye to the physical violence they experience in many homes.

My dream is that one day the people of God will begin to speak out to society, in a loud and prophetic voice, for the children – those who will never be able to speak for themselves. Children are the first victims in every society, yet the most trusting. They are those who suffer first from inhumanity, violence, famine and a multitude of social ills.

Will the church begin to declare and live out the truth that every child is a person and can grow to wholeness through the grace of God?

BOOKS FOR FURTHER READING AND REFERENCE

A Fairer Future for Children by Mia Kellmer Pringle; Macmillan

And Do Not Hinder Them; World Council of Churches

Beginnings by Maggie Durran; Celebration Publishing

Bringing Up Children in the Christian Faith by John Westerhoff III; Winston Press

Dibs: In Search of Self by Virginia M. Axline; Penguin

Happy Children by Rudolf Dreikurs; Fontana

Health Choices; Open University

Jesus and the Children by Hans-Ruedi Weber; World Council of Churches

Learning Community by John M. Sutcliffe; Denholm House Press

Living with Children 5–10; Open University

Parenting for Peace and Justice by Kathleen and James McGinnis; Orbis

Parents and Teenagers; Open University

Peoplemaking by Virginia Satir; Souvenir Press

Soul Friend by Kenneth Leech; Sheldon Press

Summerhill by A. S. Neill; Pelican

The Child in the Church; British Council of Churches

The Child, the Family and the Outside World by D. W. Winnicott; Pelican

The Needs of Children by Mia Kellmer Pringle; Hutchinson

The Parable of the Quest; General Synod Board of Education

The Pedagogy of the Oppressed by Paulo Freire; Continuum, New York

The Pre-School Child; Open University

Understanding Christian Nurture; British Council of Churches

What Do You Say to a Child When You Meet a Flower? by David P. O'Neill; Anthony Clarke Books

Your Child's Self-Esteem by Dorothy Corkville Briggs; Doubleday Dolphin